Denmark

Denmark

BY R. CONRAD STEIN

Enchantment of the World
Second Series

Children's Press®

A Division of Scholastic Inc.

NEW YORK TORONTO LONDON AUCKLAND SYDNEY
MEXICO CITY NEW DELHI HONG KONG
DANBURY, CONNECTICUT

Frontispiece: Frilandsmuseet open air museum, Lyngby, Denmark

Consultant: Jakob Stougaard-Nielsen, visiting lecturer of Danish,
University of Washington, Seattle

Please note: All statistics are as up-to-date as possible at the time of publication.

Book production by Herman Adler Design

Library of Congress Cataloging-in-Publication Data

Stein, R. Conrad.
  Denmark / by R. Conrad Stein
    p. cm. — (Enchantment of the world. Second series)
Includes bibliographical references and index.
ISBN 0-516-24213-X
  1. Denmark—Juvenile literature. [1. Denmark.] I. Title. II. Series.
  DL109.S8 2003
  948.9—dc21   2002156703

Denmark

Cover photo:
Colorful harbor
front of Nyhavn
in Copenhagen

Contents

Tórshavn

The Little Mermaid

A Kingdom of the People

DENMARK IS A MONARCHY, A COUNTRY RULED BY A KING or a queen. It is the oldest monarchy in Europe. Many Americans believe that in a monarchy the king or the queen lives in royal splendor, worlds apart from the commoners. However, if an American tourist rides a public bus past the royal palace in Copenhagen, he or she might see a surprising sight. On any given day the queen might step onboard the bus. Perhaps Her Majesty has decided to take a shopping trip. The queen pays her fare to the bus driver and takes a seat alongside the other passengers. Probably she is accompanied by a few bodyguards, but they are hardly noticed.

True, Denmark is a kingdom. Yet it is also one of the most democratic nations on earth.

Denmark is a small nation in northern Europe. The American city of Los Angeles, including its suburbs, has a greater number of residents than all of Denmark. Officially the country is named *Kongeriget Danmark* (Kingdom of Denmark). The citizens are called Danes. Copenhagen is the kingdom's capital and its largest city.

Every year millions of visitors from around the world come to Denmark. Tourists take bicycle trips through Denmark's pleasant villages, or they swim off the country's sandy white beaches. Copenhagen lures guests with a

Opposite: **Queen Margrethe, ruler of Denmark, waves to fellow Danes**

Town Hall Square is a popular visiting place for those touring Copenhagen.

Flowers bloom before stately Rosenborg Castle in Copenhagen

host of sights, including its magical amusement park, Tivoli Gardens. History abounds in Denmark. Near Copenhagen is the Kronborg Castle, which dates to the 1400s and is the place of countless legends.

Denmark is an extraordinarily clean and well-ordered country. Trains run on time. The cities have no evident slums. Homeless or terribly impoverished people are few in number. The government's tax structure takes money from the middle class and the very wealthy and uses the money to make life better for those who are less well off. Education is free for all Danish citizens, and the schools are excellent.

This is not to say that Denmark is a paradise. Danes grumble about the high prices they must pay for food, housing, and entertainment. The people are unhappy that their medical system, which once was outstanding, now suffers severe shortages of doctors and hospital facilities.

Yes, Denmark—like any other nation—faces problems. However, the country has a long and rich history. In the past it suffered through wars and military occupation, yet the Danes always maintained a surprising level of patience and cheer. Denmark is one of those special countries where tourists go to meet the people as well as to see the famous sights.

Another reason foreigners find this land so inviting can be summed up in the wonderfully Danish word *hygge*. The word defies a proper translation. Hygge simply means having fun with friends. Visitors to Denmark experience both fun and friendliness, so they choose to come back again and again.

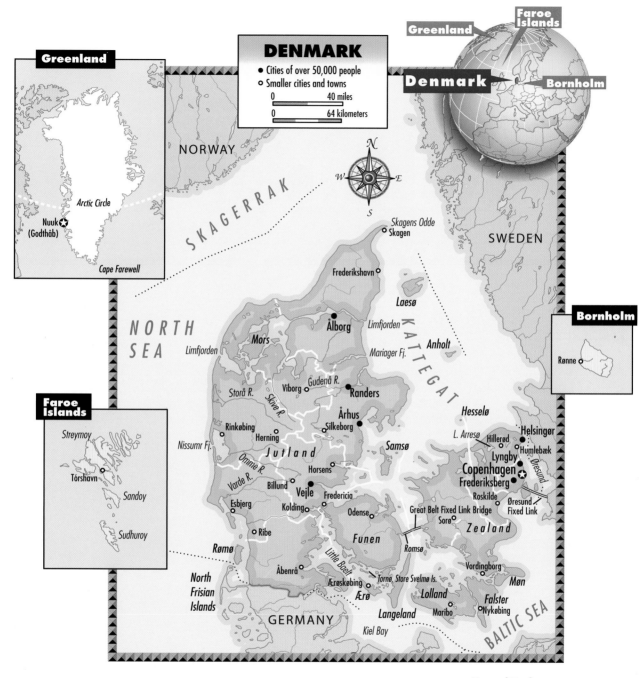

DENMARK

- Cities of over 50,000 people
- Smaller cities and towns

0   40 miles

0   64 kilometers

Greenland

Nuuk (Godthåb)

Arctic Circle

Cape Farewell

Faroe Islands

Streymoy

Tórshavn

Sandoy

Sudhuroy

Bornholm

Rønne

Greenland

Faroe Islands

Denmark

Bornholm

NORWAY

SWEDEN

GERMANY

SKAGERRAK

NORTH SEA

KATTEGAT

BALTIC SEA

Kiel Bay

Skagens Odde
Skagen

Frederikshavn

Laesø

Anholt

Ålborg

Mors

Limfjorden

Limfjorden

Mariager Fj.

Storå R.

Skive R.

Viborg

Gudenå R.

Randers

Hesselø

L. Arresø

Hillerød

Helsingør

Humlebæk

Lyngby

Copenhagen

Frederiksberg

Øresund

Rinkøbing

Herning

Silkeborg

Århus

Samsø

Jutland

Nissumr Fj.

Omme R.

Horsens

Varde R.

Billund

Vejle

Fredericia

Roskilde

Øresund Fixed Link

Esbjerg

Kolding

Odense

Great Belt Fixed Link Bridge

Sorø

Zealand

Ribe

Funen

Romsø

Rømø

North Frisian Islands

Åbenrå

Little Baelt

Ærøskøbing

Ærø

Torø, Store Svelmø Is.

Lolland

Maribo

Vordingborg

Møn

Falster

Nykøbing

Langeland

Geopolitical map of Denmark

A Land by the Sea

Denmark seen from foreign land
Looks but like a grain of sand.
Denmark as we Danes conceive it
Is so big you won't believe it.

Why not let us compromise
About Denmark's proper size?
Which will truly please us all
Since it's greater than it's small.
—Piet Hein (1905–1996), Danish poet

Look quickly at a map of Europe, and Denmark appears to be a peninsula jutting above Germany into the North Sea. Looking more closely at the map, you'll see hundreds of islands, large and small. The prominent peninsula, called Jutland, makes up 70 percent of the country's land area. In addition to Jutland, Denmark is made up of more than 400 islands. The precise number of islands depends on who's doing the counting, as some are little more than rocks poking above the waters. About 100 of Denmark's islands are inhabited.

Including all the islands, Denmark covers 16,629 square miles (43,069 square kilometers). This makes Denmark roughly the size of the American state of West Virginia. Most of Denmark's islands are clustered near the Jutland peninsula. An exception is the island of Bornholm, which lies

Opposite: **A hilltop view of Tórshavn and the sea**

A Land by the Sea   **13**

in the Baltic Sea 80 miles (129 km) east of Copenhagen and is closer to Poland than it is to Denmark.

Most Danes live on the islands. The largest island is Zealand, with a population of 2 million. The city of Copenhagen sits on Zealand's east coast. Other major islands include Funen (or Fyn), Lolland, and Falster. About 60 of the inhabited islands have fewer than 1,000 residents.

Coastal area of Funen, one of Denmark's many islands

Zealand: A Gift to the Gods

A legend claims that a Nordic goddess named Gefion once asked the king of Sweden to give her land. (The legend does not explain why a powerful goddess would have to make such a request of a mere king.) The king told Gefion she could have as much land as she could plow in one day. So, according to the story, Gefion turned her four sons into oxen and plowed the island of Zealand out of the sea. On the Copenhagen waterfront stands the immense Gefion Fountain (right) that dramatically shows the goddess driving her four oxen sons.

By the Sea

Travel in Denmark and you breathe sea air. Nowhere is one more than 35 miles (56 km) from the ocean. Denmark's only land neighbor is Germany. A human-made border about 42 miles (68 km) long separates Germany from the peninsula of Jutland. At sea its nearest neighbors are Sweden and Norway. On a clear day (and those can be rare in foggy Denmark) one can stand on the beach at Zealand and see the coast of Sweden.

Throughout its history Denmark has had close ties with Norway and Sweden. Taken together, Denmark, Norway, and Sweden are called the Scandinavian countries. They are best described as the lands

Coastline at Skagen, the northernmost point in Denmark

A Look at Denmark's Cities

With 280,000 people, Århus, on east Jutland, is Denmark's second largest city. Founded around the year 900, Århus once served as a port for Viking ships. Today it is a university town and one of Denmark's cultural centers. A well-preserved inner city hosts theaters, music halls, and fine cafés. In recent years Århus has become a magnet for immigrants from the Middle East, Africa, and Asia. Turkish merchants enliven the city's market sections.

Odense (below), which is named after the Norse god Odin, is Denmark's third largest city, with 184,000 people. Its most famous citizen is the great storyteller Hans Christian Andersen, who was born in Odense in

1805. Much of modern downtown Odense retains the fairy-tale charm associated with Andersen's genius.

Truly a fairy-tale village is Ærøskøbing on the island of Ærø. Once a prosperous merchants' town, it is now one of the most visited places in Denmark, largely because of its unique old houses. The houses on the town's main street tend to list, so they appear to be leaning on each other's shoulders. Many Ærøskøbing houses date back to the 1600s.

Ålborg (or Aalborg) (above), in north Jutland, is Denmark's fourth largest city, with 155,000 people. Ålborg's cultural scene is enhanced by a university and the lively cafés that line its main street. One of Denmark's oldest communities, Ålborg celebrated its 1,300th birthday in 1992.

where Scandinavian people live. Scandinavian people have common customs and similar languages. Some geographers include Finland in this category, but the Finns are not true Scandinavians, because their language is very different.

To better understand the geography of Denmark, it is helpful to follow what could be called the country's "belt." Beginning at Copenhagen trace a line west through the width of Zealand, cross the waters to Jutland, and then skirt the peninsula to the town of Esbjerg on Jutland's west coast. By following this belt you have passed through the middle of Denmark, and you have seen many of its population centers. Years ago such a trip would require at least two ferryboat rides. Today the beltway is connected by bridges. A train trip from Copenhagen to Esbjerg takes just over three hours.

The landscape of Denmark is mostly flat and made up of plains and low hills.

Lay of the Land

Denmark is a land of flat plains and low rolling hills. Some geographers claim Denmark is the flattest country in the world. Its highest point is a hill in Jutland called Yding Skovhøj, which rises only 568 feet (173 meters) above sea level. In a region such as New England in the United States, Denmark's highest hill would be considered a gentle rise.

Although Denmark is one of the world's smallest countries, its coastline is incredibly long. Including its islands and

Shifting sand dunes approach a lighthouse along the Jutland coast.

small bays, the coast of Denmark runs for more than 4,500 miles (7,242 km). If this coastal region were magically laid out in one straight line, that line would stretch one-sixth of the way around the earth.

Among the treasures of the coastal region are dozens of natural inlets called fjords. Many fjords have gorgeous sandy beaches. Along Jutland's north coast are great white sand dunes that drift in slow-moving waves. An old lighthouse in the region, which is partially buried by migrating dunes, now serves as the *Sandflugtmuseum* (Sand Drift Museum). The island of Møn, south of Zealand, is world famous for its coastline of chalky white cliffs.

Dramatic cliffs on the island of Møn

Fun Facts About Denmark

Census figures show that the tiny islands of Tornø, Romø, and Hesselø have only two inhabitants apiece; the island of Store Svelmø has a total population of one!

Greenland, which is part of the kingdom of Denmark, is the world's largest island.

According to *The World Factbook*, Danes have seen snowfall on Christmas only five times during the twentieth century.

Beaches on the Danish island of Bornholm have powdery white sand that is so fine it was once used in hourglasses.

Denmark does not have a single mountain.

The country has few large rivers and lakes. Still, there are a thousand or more lakes large enough to have names. Lakes are concentrated in the region called the Lake District of east Jutland. The largest lake is Lake Arresø, which covers 16 square miles (41 sq km). Denmark's longest river is Gudenå, about 100 miles (161 km) in length.

Climate

Denmark is as far north as Alaska, but it does not get anywhere nearly as cold as that American state. Ocean currents coming from as far away as the Gulf of Mexico on the other side of the Atlantic warm the country and protect it from Arctic chills. The average winter temperature in Denmark is about 32° Fahrenheit (0° Celsius). Light snows fall fifteen to twenty days in the course of a winter, but the snow usually melts quickly. On rare occasions a blizzard will strike Denmark, burying city streets and snarling traffic.

Despite these mild temperatures, don't think about swimming at a public beach when visiting Denmark in the winter. Danish winters are damp and chilly. With clouds covering the sky day after day, the winter season can be downright dismal.

In late December, Danes enjoy only a scant eight hours of daylight. Even during those daylight hours the sun is usually tucked behind thick layers of clouds. The Danish people have to fight to keep their good humor through the winter season, which begins in September and stretches into April.

By contrast, the spring and the summer are glorious. In early May, Danes cast their raincoats and hoods aside, and a person can see what his neighbor looks like again. Summer temperatures average 63°F (17°C). The people enjoy refreshing sea breezes and low humidity. Summer, with its more or less cloudless skies, lasts from May through September. Then—as all Danes know—the gray skies and damp chill of winter will settle upon their land again.

Denmark receives an average 24 inches (61 centimeters) of total precipitation (rain and melted snow) each year. Rain usually comes in the form of mist or drizzle rather than a storm. The month of June has the lightest rainfall (an average of eleven days), while November has the heaviest precipitation (eighteen days on average). Because there are no mountains, rainfall is evenly distributed throughout the land.

Conservation, Danish Style

Few people practice conservation with the fervor of the Danes. They have a small, extremely pretty country, and they are determined to keep it that way by zealously preserving their environment. Danes know that garbage dumps scar the landscape. Consequently, 64 percent of all Danish wastes are recycled. The emphasis the country places on recycling and

Denmark's Geographical Features

Area: 16,629 square miles (43,069 sq km) (not including Greenland and the Faroe Islands)

Makeup of the Land: The Jutland Peninsula constitutes 70 percent of Denmark's land area; the remaining land is made up of roughly 406 islands

Largest City: Copenhagen (1.4 million people)

Other Major Cities: Århus (280,000 people), Odense (184,000), Ålborg (155,000)

Greatest Distances: North to south, 225 miles (362 km); east to west, 250 miles (402 km)

Highest Elevation: Yding Skovhøj, 568 feet (173 m) above sea level

Lowest Elevation: Sea level along the coasts

Coastline: More than 4,500 miles (7,242 km), including all the islands

Longest River: Gudenå, about 100 miles (161 km) long

Largest Lake: Arresø, approximately 16 square miles (41 sq km)

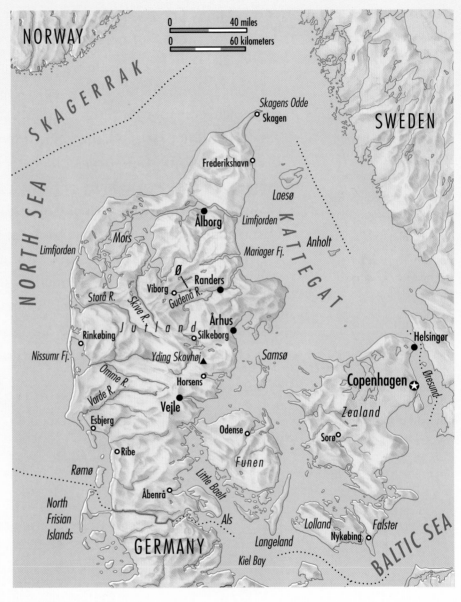

No to Nukes

The country of France is committed to nuclear power. About 75 percent of all France's electricity comes from nuclear-driven generators, the highest rate in all Europe. Neighboring Sweden also uses nuclear power. Denmark considers nuclear plants to be too dangerous. There are no nuclear generators in the country.

proper disposal of wastes is seen in Denmark's remarkably clean city streets and roadsides.

Danes also labor to keep their air pure. Power plants burning coal pollute the air. Long ago Danes replaced their coal plants with cleaner-burning natural gas to drive electric generators. Still not satisfied, the Danes have turned to the winds. In rural Denmark stand rows of high-tech windmills. Basically simple devices, a windmill consists of a giant three-blade propeller whirling on a single pedestal. Fifteen percent of Denmark's electrical power comes from windmills.

Strict laws prevent industries from dumping waste matter into rivers. Consequently, Denmark's streams run pure. The country's coastline—the pride of Denmark—is protected from development. In 1937, long before most other nations were concerned with preserving their natural beauty, the Danish

Cows graze among high-tech windmills in the farmland of Denmark.

parliament passed a law prohibiting private construction within 328 feet (100 m) of the sea. This law guarantees that the coastline is public land. Bicycle and hiking trails wind through coastal areas, giving people an unrestricted and very awe-inspiring view of the sea.

Greenland and the Faroe Islands

Danish schoolchildren delight in asking foreign visitors a trick question: What is the largest country in western Europe? The tourists will think about the question, and most will say France or Germany (France is correct). Then Danish kids shout out, "Wrong! Denmark is the biggest."

In one respect the children are correct. Denmark is western Europe's largest nation if you include Greenland and the Faroe Islands as part of its total area. Both Greenland and the Faroe Islands are possessions of the kingdom. However, Greenland and the Faroes have home rule, which means that they are completely self-governing in domestic matters, with independent governments, so most geographers do not consider them part of the Kingdom of Denmark.

Spreading over 840,000 square miles (2,175,600 sq km), Greenland is the world's biggest island. Australia is larger, but it is classified as a continent rather than an island. Greenland is about three times as big as the American state of Texas. In fact, Greenland is fifty times larger than Denmark. Yet only about 56,000 people live in Greenland, and they are concentrated along the seacoast. The island's interior is covered by a layer of ice more than a mile thick. Most Greenlanders are native Inuit who have some Danish or other Scandinavian bloodlines.

Dogs pull a sled along the frozen layer of earth in Greenland.

The Faroes are a group of eighteen islands that lie in the Atlantic Ocean roughly halfway between Iceland and the British Isles. The islands are known for their magnificent cliffs, which stand like fortresses against a constant battering from waves and fierce winds. About 45,600 people, most of them Scandinavians, live on the Faroes.

Hundreds of years ago Danes and other Scandinavians colonized Iceland, Greenland, and the Faroes. Iceland was a Danish possession until 1944, when Icelanders voted for complete independence from their mother country.

The mountainous coastline of the Faroe Islands

False Advertising

In the distant past Scandinavian people were willing to settle on the smaller of two Atlantic islands because it had a more agreeable climate. Scandinavian kings hoped to even out this settlement pattern. So the rulers gave the large island the inviting name Greenland even though it was covered with ice, and they gave the smaller place the forbidding name Iceland. The hoax did not work. More people moved to Iceland than to Greenland, and today Iceland has a population of about 278,000 compared with Greenland's 56,000.

CHAPTER

THREE

Gifts of Nature

A stork had built his nest on the roof of the last house in a little town. The mother stork was sitting on the nest with her little ones, who stuck out their little black beaks, which had not turned red yet. The father stork stood a little way off on the ridge of the roof, erect and stiff, with one leg drawn up under him. . . . One might have thought he was carved out of wood, he stood so still!
—The Danish writer Hans Christian Andersen, from his fairy tale "The Storks"

Opposite: **Summer fields bloom in Denmark's countryside.**

Denmark's forests continue to expand due to the country's conservation efforts.

FOR HUNDREDS OF YEARS THE SOIL OF DENMARK HAS BEEN farmed and farmed again. It is a crowded country, dotted with villages and towns. Given these circumstances, one would think Denmark has very little room for meadowlands and forests given over to nature. Not true. More than 1,200 species of plants thrive in Denmark. The country's rich plant life— Green Denmark—will surprise a visitor.

About 10 percent of Denmark's surface is forest-covered. Due to conservation efforts, forest land has doubled during the past hundred years. Plans are now in place to increase future forested areas by 25 percent. Denmark's forests are planted and managed as carefully as a farmer would tend crops. Laws forbid the unauthorized cutting of trees. The woodlands consist mainly of spruce, pine, maple, beech, and horse chestnut trees.

In springtime wild heather blooms in the meadows, and bright yellow rapeseed flowers appear in pastures. Sand dunes

Denmark's sand dunes are home to the vibrant beach rose.

Dutch Elm Disease

Stately old elm trees used to line the streets of Copenhagen. Then, in 1993, Dutch elm disease ravaged the land. Most of Copenhagen's 10,000 elm trees had to be cut down. City dwellers wept at the sight of the great trees being felled and hauled away.

along the west coast of Jutland explode with plant life in May and June. To prevent erosion due to coastal winds, the Danes have planted lyme and marram grasses on the dunes. These grasses have deep root systems that help hold the hills' sand in place. Also growing in sand dune regions are lovely white and pink beach roses.

One of the best places to enjoy Green Denmark is on the island of Bornholm. This, the most remote of Denmark's islands, has an amazingly abundant world of plants and trees. More than 20 percent of Bornholm's surface is tree-covered, making it Denmark's most wooded region. In the center of the island is the Almindingen forest, the country's third largest wooded area. Cherry trees abound on Bornholm, and in June their blossoms cover branches like fresh-fallen snow.

Wildlife in Denmark

In the distant past bears, elks, wolves, and a host of other wild animals made their homes in Denmark. These animals vanished as farms and villages spread over the land. It is said Denmark's last wolf was shot in the 1800s.

Every spring storks migrate to Denmark, some even nest in chimneys.

Today the Danish people work to preserve the wild animals that live in their country. Often the people simply allow the dwellers of the wilds to move into their towns and live with them as neighbors. As the Hans Christian Andersen story "The Storks" suggests, storks are village dwellers in Denmark. The stork is believed to bring good luck to a household. European storks live in Africa during the winter and migrate north in the summer months. The great birds build nests in chimneys and tend to return to the same nest each year. Each spring Danish families celebrate the return of *their* storks as they would hail the sudden arrival of old friends.

Denmark is home to an estimated forty-nine species of wild mammals. The greatest concentration of wildlife lives on the outskirts of rural villages.

Hedgehogs are welcomed guests of Danes, as they keep the insect population under control.

The largest wild mammal in Denmark is the red deer.

Found on the fringes of towns are foxes, red squirrels, rabbits, hedgehogs, and martens. Hedgehogs look like baby porcupines. Suburban gardeners encourage hedgehogs to nest in vegetable and flower patches because they eat harmful insects.

The red deer is Denmark's largest wild animal. Red deer are sometimes called the elks of Europe because they are almost as large as the North American elk. The roe deer, a smaller species, also roams freely in forested areas.

Herds of deer live in the Rold Skov National Forest in north Jutland. The Rold Skov is the nation's largest forest and its only national park. Spreading over 32 square miles (83 sq km), the park is laced with hiking trails, bike paths, and roads for horseback riding. Almost every variety of Denmark's wild animals live in this protected forestland.

Now and then a rare animal pops up in Denmark and stirs up excitement. In 1999 a moose somehow swam across the water gap from Sweden and climbed to shore on a beach in Zealand. Sadly, the moose was killed by a speeding train. A year later two young beavers were observed in a stream in Jutland. Beavers had been extinct in Denmark for hundreds of years, so it was assumed that the pair had wandered up from Germany. At last report the beavers were doing just fine.

Rold Skov, Denmark's largest forest and only national park

Great Dogs, Wrong Name

The Great Dane is a huge and lovable animal, but it is misnamed. Dog experts claim the Great Dane originated in Germany, not Denmark.

Copenhagen's Delightful Zoo

The city zoo of Copenhagen is one of the oldest and largest in Europe. It holds more than 2,500 animals, ranging from gigantic polar bears to cuddly pandas. Zoo authorities try to re-create each animal's natural environment. Thus the creatures of tropical Africa live in what looks and feels like a rainforest, while the penguins are behind glass in conditions similar to those of the South Pole.

Denmark is home to about 400 species of birds. Commonly seen birds in inland areas include coots, crows, ducks, geese, magpies, pigeons, and sparrows. Flocks of water birds, including avocets, black-winged godwits, dunlins, and ruffs fly on the coastlands. Once-common birds such as wood sandpipers and black grouse are becoming rare due to the reduction of their natural habitat.

Below left: **The coot, a bird commonly seen in Denmark**

Below right: **The avocet is usually seen along Denmark's coast.**

In inland waters swim thirty-seven species of freshwater fish. The coastal regions host an astonishing variety of marine life. Some 110 varieties of saltwater fish live off the nation's shores. Among the most plentiful are herring and plaice. Hikers along the cliffs can stop to watch seals playing on the rocks below.

The swan is Denmark's national bird.

National Symbols of Nature

The national bird of Denmark is the swan. This graceful bird is found in the Danish wilderness and in the ponds of city parks. Denmark does not have a national animal. Kids often come up with the initial ideas on these matters, and perhaps someday a group of schoolchildren will suggest an animal and the Danish parliament will adopt that animal as its national symbol. The national butterfly is the tortoise-shell, an orange butterfly with a touch of blue in its wings. Denmark is home to sixty-eight species of butterflies.

Denmark's national tree is the beech, which was introduced from North America. The national flower is the marguerite—a pretty white daisy with a yellow center; marguerites are grown in many Danish gardens.

Tortoise-shell butterfly

A Proud Past

Knud wards the land, as Christ,
The shepherd of Greece, doth then heaven.
—King Knud, the King of Denmark,
England, and Norway, 1016

MEN AND WOMEN ENTERED PRESENT-DAY DENMARK more than 100,000 years ago during the last ice age. At the time, great mountains of ice consumed much of the world's ocean waters. Because the oceans had shrunk, bands of nomadic hunters were able to walk to Denmark from what is now Norway and Sweden and even from the British Isles. However, the ice-age hunters did not establish permanent camps in Denmark.

Continuous human habitation began about 10,000 B.C.E., and sometime near 3000 B.C.E. the residents of Denmark learned to grow crops and keep animals. The ancient farmers buried their dead and marked the graves with an upright stone crossed with a capstone, like a letter T. Some of these prehistoric grave markers can still be seen in parts of the country.

In about 2000 B.C.E. people began fashioning tools from bronze, and Europe graduated from the Stone Age into the Bronze Age. The Iron Age began 1,000 years later, when Europeans discovered how to make iron tools. During the Iron Age travel and trade by sea thrived. About 500 A.D. a tribe called the Danes migrated from Sweden south to Denmark.

Opposite: **Tenth-century bronze Viking helmets**

A Treasure in Bronze

The *Nationalmuseet* (National Museum) in Copenhagen holds a wealth of bronze items once used in Denmark, including bronze horns that can still blow a tune. The most spectacular item is the 3,500-year-old Sun Chariot (right), made by Bronze Age sun worshipers. The miniature chariot, which was dug up from a farmer's field in Zealand, bears carvings of a golden sun being towed across the heavens by a horse.

The Iron Age: A Hands-On Experience

Near the village of Lejre in north Zealand stands the Lejre Historical Archaeological Research Center. Featured at the center is a reconstructed Iron Age village made up of low-lying huts with thatched roofs (right). The houses are based on excavations of Iron Age communities. Kids visiting the center learn how to paddle a dugout canoe or cook over an open fire with Iron Age utensils. For a rugged experience, Danish families volunteer to spend a week living in the huts and conducting their lives much the way people did thousands of years ago.

The Danes brought the language used in Denmark today, Danish. Years after the Danes arrived, the country became known as *Danmark* (District of the Danes).

The Sword and the Sea

In the year 789 a crew of sailors stepped off a ship in the county of Dorset, England. The sheriff of Dorset thought they were merchants and invited them into the village to see what they had to trade. The men beat the sheriff to death with clubs, raided the village for valuables, and returned to their ship. This brutal episode was England's first recorded encounter with the Vikings. In the years to come the Vikings would be the scourge of England and most of the rest of Europe.

Viking warriors came from Denmark, Norway, and Sweden. Their name probably derives from the old Scandinavian word *vik*, which means bay or inlet. They were also called Northmen or Norsemen. So many Vikings sailed to England from Denmark that the English called them Danes.

The invaders seemed to thrive on warfare. Englishmen claimed that in the heat of battle Vikings laughed like

The arrival of a Viking longship to the coast of Normandy

9th-Century Viking Invasions

Settled from Denmark   Settled from Norway

The Vikings, known for their ruthless raids, fight a fierce hand-to-hand battle.

What's in a Word?

The Norse word for warrior was *berserker*. Because the English believed a Viking went crazy with pleasure during battle, the English used the word *berserk* to mean "insane" or "violent."

madmen. Their raiding parties singled out Christian churches because they often held gold and other treasures. Churches across England uttered a special prayer, "God, deliver us from the fury of the Northmen."

How brutal were these Viking raiders? In the year 845 a Danish prince named Ragnar led 120 ships into the Seine River to attack Paris, France. The local king foolishly split his army in two and tried to fight the flotilla from both sides of the river. Ragnar and the Danes quickly subdued one of the two army groups. Then, as soldiers on the other side of the Seine watched in horror, Ragnar's men hanged all the prisoners from trees. After witnessing this mass murder, the king offered Ragnar 7,000 pounds of silver to withdraw his ships and leave Paris alone. The ransom was called *Danegelts*, or Danish money. Ragnar accepted the offer. But in future raids the Vikings often threatened a city, accepted Danegelts as ransom, and then sacked and burned the city anyway.

Though they were ruthless, it is wrong to think of the Vikings as pirates only. Traders as well as raiders, the Vikings established merchant outposts in hundreds of European ports. They were also bold explorers who ventured to the far reaches of the world. Long before the voyage of Christopher Columbus, the Vikings established villages in Greenland, Iceland, and the Faroe Islands. In the year 1002 the Norseman Leif Erickson sailed from Greenland and founded a short-lived colony he called *Vinland* (Wineland) somewhere on the northeastern coast of North America.

The Viking god of war, Odin, was prayed to by warriors entering battle.

Viking storytellers created a world of mythology that was as fabulous as that of the Greeks. The myths tell of a golden age dominated by gods and heroes. The gods created the first man from an ash tree and the first woman from an elm tree. The heavenly home of the gods was Valhalla, a great hall where the souls of warriors went after death. Mightiest of all the deities was Odin, the god of war. Upon going into battle, the Vikings prayed to Odin, imploring the god to grant them victory, or at least a noble death.

The Viking Ship Museum

An Englishman once wrote that Viking vessels looked like "dragons flying in the air." These feared Viking boats held crews of forty to fifty sailors and were sturdy enough to withstand fierce Atlantic storms. Five Viking ships are displayed at the Viking Ship Museum in the town of Roskilde on Zealand. In the eleventh century the residents of Roskilde deliberately sank the five ships to prevent an enemy fleet from approaching their harbor. The boats were discovered on the sea bottom in 1962. They were raised and restored and now stand as proud symbols of Denmark's Viking past.

In the year 950 King Harold II (also called Harald Bluetooth) united the lands of Denmark. Previously, parts of Jutland and the nearby islands were made up of small principalities ruled by minor kings or nobles. Harald Bluetooth also brought Christianity to Denmark. The new religion spread quickly, but many Danes continued to worship their ancient nordic gods in secret ceremonies.

Sore Loser

King Knud (994?–1035) is famed—or ill famed—for his behavior during a chess game. While playing with Ulf the Jarl, a relative, Knud made a foolish move and lost his knight. The king grew so furious that he sent a man out with orders to murder his chess opponent. The man discovered Ulf the Jarl praying in a chapel and ran him through with a sword. It is not known if anyone ever again played chess with King Knud.

"London Bridge Is Falling Down, Falling Down..."

Every child who grows up in an English-speaking country learns the ancient song about London Bridge. Some historians believe the song dates back to a raid on England by Danish Vikings in the year 1014. At the height of the raid the Danes pulled down the wooden bridge the English had built over the Thames River in London. Then, while standing over the wreckage of the bridge, the Danes wrote a poem praising their destructive act.

For long periods Danish Vikings controlled a large section of England that they called the *Danelaw*. In 1013 the Dane Sweyn Forkbeard crowned himself king of England and Denmark. Sweyn's son Canute (also spelled "Knut" and "Knud") further expanded Danish authority by becoming king of Denmark and Norway as well as England.

Danish rule over England ended in 1042. Most of the Danes who lived in England simply melted in with the population, and their descendants remain there to this day. Danish withdrawal from England marked the end of the Viking era. Today those years of sword and sea are romanticized in novels and in film.

Minister to King Valdemar I, Bishop Absalon founded the fortress village of present-day Copenhagen.

A Mighty Empire

King Valdemar I (the Great) took the throne in 1157. The king was aided by a minister named Absalon, a scholarly priest who was equally comfortable ordering armies into battle and sitting quietly at home reading the Bible. In the late 1100s Bishop Absalon built a castle at a tiny fishing village on the

eastern shores of Zealand. Absalon looked upon the village as a future naval fortress as well as a trading port. It was named *København* (Merchants' Haven or Merchants' Harbor), and today it is known to the world as Copenhagen.

Danes of the time saw the hand of God—angry or gentle—everywhere. In 1350 the bubonic plague, called the Black Death, struck Denmark and most of the rest of Europe. One out of every three Europeans died in the terrible epidemic. The plague was caused by fleas on rats; however, priests told the people they were being punished by God. Several years later, through some odd shifting of currents, great schools of herring appeared off Denmark's coasts. The tiny fish were so plentiful they could be scooped into boats with shovels. Danes now had plenty to eat, and they dropped to their knees to thank God for the gift from the sea.

Queen Margrethe I allied Denmark, Norway, and Sweden, creating a new government, the Union of Kalmar.

A champion of Danish expansion was Queen Margrethe I, who ruled beginning in 1375. Early in her reign Denmark and the other Scandinavian countries were threatened by the Hanseatic League, an alliance of German commercial towns. To counter German power, Queen Margrethe I united Denmark, Norway, and Sweden under one government. The government, formed in 1397, was called the Union of Kalmar after the Swedish town where the alliance was formalized. Denmark was the wealthiest and the most populous of the three countries and dominated the alliance. The great Scandinavian compact included Greenland, Iceland, and the Faroe Islands.

In theory the Union of Kalmar lasted for 126 years. But in fact the alliance lost much of its strength when Queen Margrethe I died in 1412. Margrethe was a remarkable diplomat. With her death the dream of Scandinavian unity ended. Sweden pulled out of the alliance in 1523. Denmark and Sweden then clashed in a series of bloody wars.

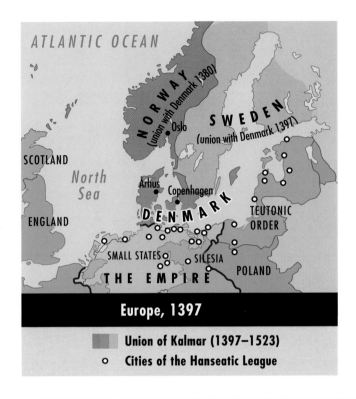

Europe, 1397

Union of Kalmar (1397–1523)

o   Cities of the Hanseatic League

Goose Tower

In 1368 King Valdemar IV, Queen Margrethe's father, erected an unusual tower at the city of Vordingborg in southern Zealand. The tower was topped by a golden goose flapping its wings as if cackling in anger. Conspicuously, the goose statue faced south—toward Germany. Today the tower is a tourist attraction in Vordinsborg, and visitors climb its 101 steps to get a breathtaking view of the sea and the town.

**Danish painting of a
Reformation church**

The Reformation

For more than 1,000 years Europeans had been followers of
the Catholic faith. Then in 1517, the German monk Martin
Luther nailed a piece of paper to the door of a church and
started a religious revolution. Written on the paper was a list
of demands for changes in the church, or reform of its practices. One of those time-honored practices was selling
indulgences (the forgiveness of sins) to wealthy patrons.
Luther led a movement called the Reformation that shook the
Old World to its religious foundations.

In less than forty years half of the people of Europe abandoned Catholicism and adopted various Protestant faiths.
Protestantism developed mostly in northern Europe, while
southern Europe remained Catholic. Religious upheaval during the Reformation triggered a terrible clash called the

Thirty Years' War, which was fought from 1618 to 1648 between many European states and the Holy Roman Empire. The most bitter fighting took place in Germany, where thousands of people were killed, cities were destroyed, and art and culture were set back hundreds of years.

Denmark had converted to Lutheranism in the 1530s. The transition to the new religion was painful. Denmark was gripped by civil war, and the nation was swept into the horrors of other wars raging in Europe. Yet the majority of Danes happily embraced the Lutheran church. The Reformation meant that no longer were church services conducted in Latin, a language only the clergy understood. Now hymnbooks and the Bible were printed in Danish. Denmark became a Lutheran state, as it is today.

Small Country, Great Minds

Night after night the Danish astronomer Tycho Brahe (1546–1601) observed the planets as they moved through the sky. He had to use his naked eye because telescopes had not been developed at the time. King Christian IV granted Brahe land on the island of Ven (also called Hven) to perform his studies. The celebrated German astronomer Johannes Kepler once worked as his assistant. After a study that lasted many years, Brahe drew up a vastly improved map of the solar system. However, not everyone was pleased with Brahe's work. The astronomer once fought a sword duel with a Danish nobleman who cut off a piece of Brahe's nose. Brahe fashioned a replacement nose from gold and wore it to cover his wound.

In 1588 a ten-year-old boy, Christian IV, became king and ruled for the next sixty years. No king of Denmark was more

Copenhagen grew and prospered during the reign of Christian IV.

beloved. He danced at peasants' weddings and worked alongside them in the fields at harvest time. Copenhagen became one of Europe's most marvelous capitals during Christian's reign. Many famous buildings that grace Copenhagen today—the Rosenborg Castle, the Round Tower, and the Børsen market—were built on King Christian's orders. Christian IV dreamed of bringing Sweden back into the fold with Denmark and Norway, but in this effort he failed miserably. Sadly, wars with Sweden dragged on and on.

Almost constant warfare drained the Danish treasury and forced the upper classes to pay high taxes. When the noblemen refused to pay, King Frederick III (who ruled from 1648 to 1670) instituted absolute monarchy. In 1665 a new constitution (called the Royal Act) was written, giving the king virtually all the nation's political power. So mighty was the king of Denmark that no one was permitted to put the crown on his head. During coronations the king was required to crown himself.

The Crown Jewels and a Curiosity

Denmark's crown jewels are on display in Copenhagen's Rosenborg Castle. Prized among this collection are the Crown of the Absolute Monarch, a headpiece studded with precious stones, and the magnificent Sword of State, which dates to 1551. Guides point to two less glittering objects that once belonged to the flamboyant King Christian IV. During a naval battle in 1644, King Christian was hit in the eye by a shell fragment. Undaunted, the king pulled the fragment out of his eye and later fashioned it into a pair of earrings that he gave to his girlfriend.

Though kings reigned supreme, Danish commoners made strides in the 1700s. The system of serfdom, in which the landlords virtually owned peasant farmers, ended. Peasants were allowed to move from barrackslike central farmhouses and to build family-size dwellings. Large estates were broken up, and small farms established. The Danish countryside took the character it has today—a patchwork of family-owned farms. In 1814 Denmark was the first country in the world to make grade-school education mandatory for all children.

Europe plunged into the Napoleonic Wars, a bloody series of campaigns that were fought from 1796 to 1815. Great Britain and France were the primary combatants in the Napoleonic Wars. Denmark had little to gain by joining either side, but the kingdom could not avoid being in the middle of the gigantic power struggle. Reluctantly, Denmark

The British fleet arrive in Copenhagen harbor April 1801 and destroy the Danish fleet.

NORWAY
SWEDEN
North Sea
DENMARK
NETHERLANDS
UNITED KINGDOM
BELGIUM
GERMAN EMPIRE
RUSSIAN EMPIRE
FRANCE
SWITZERLAND
AUSTRO-HUNGARIAN EMPIRE
ITALY
SERBIA
ROMANIA
BULGARIA
MONTENEGRO
ALBANIA
SPAIN
GREECE
OTTOMAN EMPIRE
Mediterranean Sea

World War I, 1914–1918

Allied powers   Neutrals
Central powers   .... State borders within empires

sided with France and paid a heavy price. In 1801 and again in 1807 a British fleet sailed into Copenhagen harbor and bombarded the city. The end of the Napoleonic Wars brought major border changes to Denmark. After four centuries of Danish rule, Norway withdrew from Denmark and became part of Sweden in 1814. Fifty years later Denmark lost its southern provinces of Schleswig and Holstein to Germany.

Thanks to their school system, the Danes were among the best-educated people on earth. An ever-growing middle class enjoyed comfort and security. In 1849 a new constitution established a parliament with two chambers. Denmark now had an elected government, and the absolute power wielded by the kings diminished.

The Twentieth Century

World War I broke out in Europe in 1914. During the war, soldiers— English, French, American, and German—lived in muddy trenches while machine guns and fast-firing artillery took a ghastly toll of lives. Denmark declared neutrality in World War I, and Danish youth were spared the horrors of the trenches.

The kingdom was not spared the Great Depression that struck in the 1930s. The Great Depression was a worldwide economic slowdown triggered by the collapse of the United States stock market in 1929. In Denmark farm prices dropped. In 1933 unemployment reached record levels. The Depression destabilized many countries, including Germany. The German people, in the grip of poverty, put their trust in the fiery speaker Adolf Hitler. After becoming Germany's leader in 1933, Hitler launched a massive program of rebuilding his nation's military might.

Germany attacked Poland on September 1, 1939, thereby launching World War II. Once more Denmark declared neutrality. This time, however, German troops invaded Denmark,

German advance guards enter Danish territory in April 1940.

Europe in World War II, 1939–1945

- Occupied by Germany
- Axis (German) ally
- Allied power
- Neutral power

in April 1940. The Danes did not fight back, as they knew a battle against the mighty German war machine would be futile. Many observers concluded that the Danes were simply too civilized to fight.

For five years during World War II, the Kingdom of Denmark was occupied by German soldiers. The Danes resisted their occupiers in novel ways. The Nazis ordered all Danish Jews to wear armbands bearing the Star of David so that they could be easily identified. The day after the order King Christian X walked the streets of Copenhagen wearing the Star of David. Soon thousands of ordinary Danes donned armbands, and the Nazis were unable to tell Jew from non-Jew. During the course of the occupation, courageous Danish boat crews smuggled 6,000 Danish Jews, practically the entire Jewish population, out of Denmark and into neutral Sweden.

The Museum of the Danish Resistance

Copenhagen's Museum of the Danish Resistance (*Frihedsmuseet*) tells how Danish men and women frustrated their Nazi overlords during World War II. On display are copies of newspapers that the Germans banned. About 180 illegal underground papers were printed regularly. Often the newspapers were distributed by schoolkids who hid them in bicycle baskets under a stack of books. The museum also covers the thorny subject of Danish government leaders who cooperated with the Germans during the war years.

At the conclusion of World War II, a period of tensions called the cold war emerged. The cold war pitted the communist world (headed by the Soviet Union) against the non-communist world (headed by the United States). Denmark sided with the United States. In 1949 Denmark was one of twelve nations that joined the North Atlantic Treaty Organization (NATO), a military alliance aimed at curbing aggression by the Soviet Union. The cold war ended in the late 1980s with the collapse of communism in Russia and eastern Europe.

In 1953 Danish voters approved a new constitution that established a one-house parliament and abolished the "upper" house, a holdover of the onetime Danish upper classes. The constitution also ended a long-standing "kings only" rule and allowed a female to inherit the throne. Because of this constitution, the very popular Queen Margrethe II was able to take royal office on January 15, 1972.

As the economy grew, the country's industries faced a labor shortage. In the late 1960s Denmark relaxed its laws on immigration and permitted many "guest workers" from Turkey and Pakistan to enter the country. Later, refugees came from Somalia and Ethiopia. Immigration peaked in 1995 when more than 28,000 newcomers arrived.

Denmark entered the twenty-first century as one of the most stable democracies on earth. Of course the nation is not free of problems. Taxes are high, the economy is subject to swings, and people complain that their once-outstanding health-care system is eroding. Still, Danes look forward to a bright future. In many ways tiny Denmark is the envy of the world.

CHAPTER

FIVE

The Monarch and the Parliament

D ENMARK IS A CONSTITUTIONAL MONARCHY. THIS MEANS it has a monarch, a king or a queen, but the monarch's powers are limited by the country's constitution. The constitution gives the everyday power of government to the parliament. Queen Margrethe II of Denmark is respected and loved by the people. She reigns, but she does not rule.

Opposite: **Once home to the Danish royals, Christianborg Palace in Copenhagen now houses Parliament.**

Meet Queen Margrethe II

A handful of Danes wish to end the monarchy because they believe it is an old-fashioned institution. Yet even those antimonarchy Danes would willingly elect Queen Margrethe II as the nation's prime minister. In Denmark she is revered as the mother of the land. And what a talented mother! Queen Margrethe II is an artist whose paintings command top prices at galleries. All the income she earns from her paintings is donated to charity. She recently was charmed by J. R. R. Tolkein's book *Lord of the Rings* and drew illustrations for a Danish edition.

The queen was born on April 16, 1940. This was a dark time in Denmark, as German armies had invaded the land just a week before her birth. During the occupation years the baby Margrethe was a delight in the eyes of Danish men and women. Today Queen Margrethe II is the mother of two sons and is a grandmother. TV cameras follow her everywhere, even on vacation when she skis in Norway or picks grapes in France. Of course she is loved, but there is another reason the Danes like to look at her on TV: The queen is a fan of funny-looking hats.

The Danish parliament is responsible for passing new laws and removing old ones.

The Danish parliament, called the *Folketing*, is made up of one body, or house. The Folketing has 179 members who are elected to four-year terms. The parliament is a legislative body, meaning its members pass new laws and rescind, or remove, old laws. The majority political party or group of parties elects the prime minister, who acts somewhat like the president of Denmark.

Danish prime minister Anders Fogh Rasmussen

Politician, Beware the Ombudsman

A citizen who has a complaint against the government will take that complaint to the ombudsman. An ombudsman is sort of a super-inspector over all government functions. The idea of having a powerful inspector is a Danish creation that has been copied by governments in many other countries.

The ombudsman (who might very well be a woman) is appointed by parliament to investigate any unfair practices or abuse by the government. Ministers of parliament must pay heed to the ombudsman, who serves as a watchdog over Danish authorities. The Danish constitution included the election of at least one ombudsman in 1953.

The prime minister and his cabinet remain in office only as long as their political parties can muster enough votes to keep them there. Parliament may call for new elections even before the four-year terms of the members expire. In modern Denmark as many as ten political parties run candidates for office. Therefore, it is virtually impossible for one party to maintain a majority. So parties or party leaders seek the votes of rival parties and form a coalition in order to make new laws. Given the size of the Danish parliament, a coalition of at least ninety votes is needed to pass a measure. Politics is often called the art of compromise. In Denmark, with multiple political parties, compromise is essential.

All Danish citizens eighteen and older are allowed to vote. In parliamentary elections about 85 percent of Denmark's voters regularly go to polling places and cast their ballots. This is one of the highest voter turnout rates in the world.

Denmark is divided into the borough of Fredericksburg, the city of Copenhagen, and fourteen counties, all of which have elected government officials. The counties are subdivided into 275 municipal governments that are usually

NATIONAL GOVERNMENT OF DENMARK

Executive Branch

MONARCH (CHIEF OF STATE)	PRIME MINISTER (HEAD OF GOVERNMENT)

CABINET

Legislative Branch

PARLIAMENT
(179 MEMBERS)

Judicial Branch

SUPREME COURT
(15 JUDGES)

Thou Shalt Not Kill

Petty crime such as public drunkenness and bicycle theft has soared in recent years, but Denmark is one of the world's safest nations. In 1999 Denmark recorded forty-eight homicides. The American city of Chicago, which has half of the population of Denmark, had 641 murders in the same period.

served by a mayor and a town council. Denmark's highest court is the Supreme Court, which is made up of fifteen judges. Two other high courts are headed by fifty judges. Local governments, such as municipalities, are called *Nœrdemokrati* ("close democracy").

A Contentious Election

Immigration was a hotly debated issue during the election of November 2001. For nine years a coalition of liberal parties held sway over the parliament. The liberals wanted no change in immigration policies. Two major parties made up the opposition conservative coalition. The conservatives advocated tightening up Danish laws regarding immigration.

The 2001 election was a solid victory for the conservatives, as they won ninety-eight seats in parliament. Immigration was far from the only issue argued during the campaign. The conservatives also promised to reduce taxes. But the new prime minister, Anders Fogh Rasmussen, made clear his stand on the immigration issue: "We have to make stricter laws so that fewer foreigners come to Denmark."

Danish society was under no threat of being torn apart by arguments over immigration during the 2001 elections. The fact that politicians peacefully debated immigration policies and people freely voted their choice meant Danish democracy was strong. And the 2001 contest was notable in that a Dane with an immigrant background was elected to parliament. No other immigrant had ever won office before. Naser Khader, who was born in Syria, won a seat in parliament and proclaimed, "It is a great victory for me and for the immigration policy in Denmark."

Syrian-born Naser Khader, first immigrant ever to win a seat in the Danish parliament

The Danish Flag

The Danish flag is called the *Dannebrog*, the Cloth of the Danes. It is the oldest national flag in the world. In fact, the Dannebrog is so old its origin is the stuff of legends. According to legend, the flag made its first appearance as the Danes fought an Estonian army in the year 1219. Danish troops were losing a bloody battle when all at once a beautiful red flag with a white cross fell miraculously upon the battlefield. A voice from the sky, speaking in Danish, said if the troops raised the banner they would win the battle. The Danes seized the flag, and victory was theirs. Since that time the red-and-white Dannebrog has been Denmark's national flag.

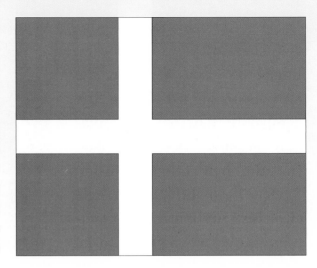

The Welfare State at Work

The beloved Danish clergyman and hymn writer Bishop Nikolai Frederik Severin Grundtvig (1783–1872) once wrote, "In terms of riches we shall have come a long way when few have too much and fewer still have too little." These words are often quoted to describe Denmark's modern welfare state. Because of taxes "few have too much." Tax-supported programs provide for the needs of the poor, and therefore "fewer still have too little." This balance between taxes and social welfare has created a comfortable and secure society.

Enter a large supermarket in Copenhagen and you will see baggers and check-out clerks hard at work. The baggers and clerks earn very little by Danish standards, yet about 40 percent of their wages will be taken away as taxes. In the United States a supermarket bagger pays less than 20 percent in taxes.

The owner of the Danish supermarket earns considerably more than the clerks. But high earnings mean a higher tax bracket. Consequently, the owner must pay more than half of his or her income in taxes.

Denmark has managed, for the most part, to eliminate poverty within its borders. Over the years the people have created a society with an economic ladder. A handful of wealthy Danes live at the top of the ladder. Less well-off citizens reside on the bottom. The vast majority of the people are crowded onto the middle steps. The government tries valiantly to prevent individuals or families from falling below the bottom step.

Several studies say that Danes are the most heavily taxed people on earth. In addition to income taxes, Danes pay a value-added tax (VAT) of 25 percent on all purchases they make. Because of the VAT, a child's winter coat that would cost $50 in American money has an actual price of $62.50 at the clothing store. These taxes drain budgets and make it hard for families to save money.

But why should the average Dane living in the welfare state be overly concerned about money in the bank? Look again at the supermarket. If the bagger or the clerk gets sick, he or she goes to the doctor free of charge. Perhaps the illness is severe and requires hospitalization. Financially this is no problem. Hospital stays, too, are paid for by the government, and all Danish workers have generous sick-leave pay. Also, public schools are outstanding, and they are tuition-free even at the university level. In fact, college students are even paid to go to school. Full-time students at universities receive as

Generous Danes

Denmark gives more aid per capita (meaning per individual within the population) to developing nations than does any other country in the world. Of this development aid, 60 percent goes to Africa, 30 percent to Asia, and 10 percent to Central America.

The Danish National Anthems

Denmark actually has two national anthems. The one most often heard, "There Is a Lovely Land," celebrates the country itself. The other anthem, "King Christian Stood by the Lofty Mast," is the anthem of the Danish royal family and is played when the queen makes an official visit to a Danish school or a government office. Here are the words to "There Is a Lovely Land," which has been used as the country's national anthem since 1844:

There is a lovely land
With spreading, shady beeches
Near Baltic's salty strand.
Its hills and valleys gently fall,
Its ancient name is Denmark
And it is Freya's hall.

There in the ancient days
The armored Vikings rested
Between their bloody frays.
Then they went forth the foe to face,
Now found in stone-set barrows,
Their final resting place.

The land is still as fair
The sea as blue around it,
And peace is cherished there.
Strong men and noble women still
Uphold their country's honour
With faithfulness and skill.

Praise the king and country with might
Bless every Dane at heart
For serving with no fright.
The Viking kingdom for Danes is true
With fields and waving beeches
By a sea so blue.

much as $400 a month from the government to help pay for their meals and rent.

True, there are disadvantages to Denmark's welfare state. Once more return to the supermarket example. High taxes make it very difficult for an ambitious bagger to save up enough money to buy his or her own supermarket. The Danish system provides workers with security from infancy through old age. The tax structure, however, gives the average Dane reduced opportunities to become wealthy through business enterprise. Still, the vast majority of Danes are satisfied with their system.

Government in Greenland and the Faroes

Greenland and the Faroe Islands are not colonies—Danes shudder when they hear that word. Colonies are thought of as captive countries whose people resent the rule of a foreign master. The people of these two provinces in the Atlantic keep close ties to Denmark because they choose to do so. The two provinces are almost the same as Danish states except they are not attached to the mainland.

Greenland has two seats in the Danish parliament, and the Faroe Islands also have two. Both provinces have their own local governments. Under the Danish Home Rule Act they are completely self-governing in domestic matters such as the administration of school systems and raising taxes. The status of Greenland is unlikely to change soon, but many people in the Faroe Islands desire independence. Elections are regularly held in the Faroes, and the islanders can achieve independence simply by voting for the measure.

Copenhagen: Did You Know This?

"Wonderful, wonderful Copenhagen, friendly old girl of a town." This song highlighted a tuneful 1952 American-made movie called *Hans Christian Andersen.* Copenhagen residents must have enjoyed that long-ago musical film because on dozens of buildings are signs proclaiming the English words "Wonderful Copenhagen!" In fact, "Wonderful Copenhagen" is the name of the city's government-run tourist agency.

Most tours of Copenhagen begin in the *Rådhuspladsen* (City Hall Square). The square lies near the city's central train station and the world-famous amusement park Tivoli Gardens. Statues of polar bears appear to be climbing near the city hall rooftop. The great white bears represent Denmark's unity with Greenland. During the day City Hall Square is crowded with schoolkids shepherded by their teachers. Copenhagen's greatest historical sites are clustered here, and classes take regular outings at the square.

For an enjoyable walk, stroll along Strøget, which is advertised as the "world's largest pedestrian mall." Along this pedestrian-only walkway are storefronts that sell T-shirts and jewelry shops that offer necklaces and bracelets worth hundreds of thousands of dollars. Street musicians and clowns entertain the strollers.

Hundreds of restaurants line the sidewalk. Many of these restaurants are fast-food places, including several McDonald's, and older Danes deplore the "hamburgerization" of their central city.

Copenhagen is called the City of Towers because of the church towers that pierce its skyline. One spire, called the *Rundetaarn* (Round Tower), is the source of a dozen stories. Built in 1637 as an astronomical observatory, the Rundetaarn rises as high as a modern eight-story building. To reach the top, one walks up a spiral ramp that winds around the tower's inner core. Czar Peter the Great of Russia visited this tower in 1716 and promptly rode his horse up the ramp. The czar was followed by his wife, who dashed up the ramp in a horse-drawn coach.

Amalienborg Palace (below) is the official residence of the royal family. Look up at the spires; if the flag is flying, it means the queen is home. Thousands of Danes cram the square every April 16 (the queen's birthday) to see her wave from the balcony. Many wings of the palace are open to the public, and tour groups admire the artwork inside. Every day at noon a colorful changing-of-the-guard ceremony takes place outside the palace doors.

The Danish parliament meets at Christiansborg Palace. The present building is about 100 years old, but there has been a palace on this spot since the year 1167.

Christiansborg Palace also houses the prime minister's office and the chambers of the Danish supreme court. When visiting Christiansborg, all guests must take off their shoes and put on special slippers to protect the delicate floors.

On Copenhagen's waterfront stands one of the most familiar pieces of sculpture in the world. In 1837 Hans Christian Andersen wrote the fairy tale of the Little Mermaid. The mermaid's statue (below), which was put up in 1913, made Copenhagen the fairy-tale capital of the world. The delicate sea-girl sits on a rock just a few yards from dockside. She gazes forlornly at crowds of admirers. Her story is a sad one. She traded her golden hair and her beautiful voice for human legs to replace her fishlike fins. With human legs she hoped to win the heart of a prince with whom she was hopelessly in love. But the prince abandoned the mermaid, leaving her on the waterfront to wait forever for his return. At least these days she has the company of thousands of shutterbugs. The Little Mermaid is the most photographed object in all of Denmark.

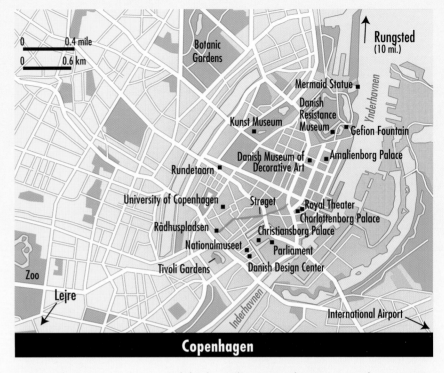

While the Little Mermaid's story is sad, so too is the series of attacks on her statue. In 1984 her right arm was amputated. In 1964 and again in 1998 her head was sawed off. These outrages were committed at night by senseless vandals. Luckily the mold made by the sculptor, Edvard Eriksen, was preserved, and workers were able to faithfully re-create the statue after each assault.

Location: The eastern side of Zealand, the largest of Denmark's 406 islands.

Population: 1.4 million people, including its near suburbs.

Founded: Officially the city was founded in the year 1167 by Bishop Absalon, but there was a fishing village at the site long before that date.

Name in Danish: *København*, meaning "merchants' harbor" or "merchants' haven."

The Danish
Economy

DENMARK HAS FEW NATURAL RESOURCES SUCH AS IRON or coal upon which industrial power is built. Yet the people enjoy a high standard of living. The source of this success lies both in the Danish genius for science and invention and with the country's diligent workforce.

Opposite: **Denmark's farms produce enough food for 15 million people.**

Products of the Farms

In 1960, 200,000 farms operated in Denmark. By the year 2000, some 60,000 working farms remained. As is true in most of Europe, Danish farmers have moved to the cities to take industrial jobs. Still, Denmark's farms produce enough food to feed the people at home and to ship tons of produce to foreign trading partners. Each year farms in Denmark grow enough food to feed 15 million people. This means the average family farm could supply food to 225 hungry people in the world. Farms grow crops despite the fact that Danish soil lacks nutrients and needs the heavy use of fertilizer. Farming in Denmark is, by necessity, mechanized and high tech. The farmer must be as much an engineer as a person of the soil.

Young and old alike work at haymaking.

An abundance of cattle produces more beef than is needed in Denmark.

More than two-thirds of the country's total land area is devoted to farms. The average farm is about 100 acres (40 hectares) in size, and most are family-owned. However, small-scale farming is not a profitable business. Many Danish farmers get up long before dawn, tend to their farm chores, and then dash off to a nearby town or village to work another job. The farms are victims of their own success. They produce more grain and beef than they can sell, and this overabundance drives down prices. Also, the farmer must spend huge sums on tractors, mechanized equipment, and fertilizers.

Farm cooperatives help ease the farmers' lot. In 1864 Danes formed the nation's first dairy cooperative. Today the pork cooperative alone has 60,000 members. Farmers in cooperatives pool their money to buy expensive harvesting machinery that all members can use. The cooperatives own companies that distribute farm produce, and they buy seed grains in bulk to drive down costs. Finally, the cooperatives provide friendly places for farmers to get together and have parties and other events.

Danish-made butter, cheese, and ice cream are highly prized throughout Europe. About 80 percent of Danish dairy products are sold abroad. Each year 21 million pigs are raised on Danish farms. Danish hams and bacon are thought of as the tastiest in the world. Animal feed is grown on fields surrounding the farms. Aside from livestock feed, farmers grow barley, potatoes, and sugar beets.

More than half of all Danish dairy products are sold overseas.

More than 20 million pigs are raised in Denmark, producing delicious hams and bacon.

Strawberries Sold on the Honor System

Farmers on the island of Ærø grow juicy strawberries. During the harvest season the farm families work in the fields and leave baskets of strawberries on the front steps of their houses. Each basket has a sign stating its price. Customers are expected to take a basket and leave the proper amount of money on the step. Ærø farmers have been using this honor system for many years, and customers never cheat.

Throughout history the Danish people have farmed the sea. Ages ago herring were used as currency and traded in markets for grain. Danish fishing boats today regularly haul in up to 2 million tons of fish a year. Cod, herring, and mackerel are the common fish caught off Denmark's shores. The city of Esbjerg is the nation's chief fishing port.

A Danish fishing boat in Esbjerg harbor with the day's catch

Weights and Measures

Denmark, as is true of most of Europe, uses the metric system. An American traveler in Denmark need keep only a few things in mind: a kilometer is about five city blocks in length, a liter of soda is about the same as three cans, a kilogram of cheese weighs 2.2 pounds. Temperatures are given on the Celsius scale. Water freezes at zero degrees Celsius, so if the thermometer reads 0° or below, that means it's mighty cold outside.

Products of Industry

Danish factories produce home electronics, silverware, and fancy porcelain dishes. One company, Danfoss, is a world leader in the production of heating and refrigeration controls. More Danes (about 16,600) work for Danfoss than for any other industrial firm in the country. Danish-made furniture is

The Wonderful World of Legos

During the depression of the 1930s a Danish carpenter named Ole Kirk Christiansen lost his job. To earn money, Christiansen made wooden toys and peddled them town to town from his bicycle basket. In a moment of genius he hit upon the idea of fashioning wooden bricks with holes and studs that allowed them to interlock. Thus Legos (which are now made of plastic) were born. The word comes from the Danish words *leg godt*, which mean "play well." Mathematicians have determined that Legos bricks can be twisted, locked, and combined in 102,981,500 ways. The company is still under family control, and it runs the fabulous Legoland amusement park (left) in central Jutland. Kids visiting Legoland ride trains and boats made from Lego bricks. Each year more than 1 million people come to Legoland, which lies near the town of Billund.

Resources

Intensive farming
Mostly animal farming
Animal farming, fodder crops
Pasture
Forest/brush
Wasteland

L Limestone
N Natural gas *
O Oil *
S Salt

* Mostly in Danish sector of the North Sea

valued throughout the world. The Danes also make ships, electrical engines, medicines, clothing, and toys. More than half of the nation's factories are concentrated in the Copenhagen area.

Food-processing firms combine agriculture with industry. Factories turn raw milk into butter and cheese. Denmark is one of the leading exporters of canned ham in the world. Other factories freeze and can fish. Denmark is world famous for its beer. The huge Carlsberg brewery has operated in Copenhagen for more than 150 years.

Wells in the North Sea provide the Danish economy with petroleum and natural gas. Because Denmark

Danish beer has been brewed at the Carlsberg brewery for more than 150 years.

What Denmark Grows, Makes, and Mines

Agriculture (2000 est.)

Wheat	4,693,000 metric tons
Barley	3,980,000 metric tons
Sugar beets	3,345,000 metric tons

Manufacturing (2000 est.) *(exports value in millions kroner)*

Machinery and transportation equipment	112,575 DK
Miscellaneous manufactured articles	74,142 DK
Chemicals and related products	68,196 DK

Mining (2000 est.)

Natural gas	9,700,000 metric tons
Limestone	950,000 metric tons
Salt (unrefined)	605,000 metric tons

has no iron or coal deposits, mining is not a major industry. Chalk and limestone for making cement are mined in Denmark, however. Mines on the island of Bornholm yield the clay used in porcelain and fine chinaware.

Women employees account for nearly half of the Danish workforce.

A Look at the Workers

Denmark has a workforce of 2.9 million people. For every ten male workers there are nine females on the job. Few other countries in the world have such a large percentage of working women. All workers enjoy generous benefits. The average Dane has five weeks paid vacation a year (compared to two weeks in the United States), and in Denmark a person works thirty-seven hours a week (forty hours is the average workweek in the United States).

A service worker performs a service for customers rather than manufacturing a product. A waitress at a restaurant is a service worker, as is a teacher or a doctor. About 72 percent of Danes are classified as service workers. Manufacturing, transportation, and construction employ 25 percent of the Danish workforce, and 3 percent are farmers.

Transportation and Communications

Denmark has 1,775 miles (2,857 km) of railroad tracks. The passenger railroad system is almost all government-owned and offers fast service from city to city. About 44,400 miles (71,455 km) of paved roads crisscross the country; 3,000 miles (4,828 km) of them are considered major highways, while the remaining are classified as secondary roads. Denmark has twenty-eight airports with paved runways. The busiest field is Copenhagen International Airport, which serves 18.1 million passengers each year.

About 260 miles (418 km) of canals and other waterways

Denmark has more than 3,000 miles of major highways.

accommodate shipping. Major ports and harbors include Åbenrå, Ålborg, Århus, Copenhagen, Esbjerg, Fredericia, Kolding, Odense, Rønne (on the island of Bornholm), and Vejle. Danish shipping companies operate more than 340 cargo vessels. Ferryboats go from island to island carrying up to 2,000 people and 400 cars. Vacationers take an eight-hour ferryboat ride from Copenhagen to the island of Bornholm. Ferries make regular runs between Copenhagen and Oslo, Norway, a trip that takes sixteen hours.

In recent years bridges have revolutionized travel in Denmark. The Great Belt Fixed Link was completed in 1998 and connects the island of Zealand to the island of Funen. Both a bridge and a tunnel, the system took ten years to complete. It was perhaps Denmark's greatest engineering feat. Previously a traveler had to take a one-hour ferryboat ride between Zealand and Funen. Now trains whisk passengers over the waters in less than ten minutes. In effect, the bridge has made the small nation of Denmark even smaller.

Due to Denmark's proximity to the sea, more than 340 cargo ships operate out of the country.

Øresund Bridge is part of a bridge-tunnel between Denmark and Sweden.

From an international point of view, a bridge connecting Denmark to Sweden is Scandinavia's most remarkable achievement. Completed in 1999, the 10-mile (16-km) structure links Denmark to the city of Malmö in Sweden. It is officially called the Øresund Train-road, Bridge-tunnel Fixed Link. Popularly, it is called the Øresund Bridge. Via the bridge, a train passenger can go from Copenhagen to Malmö, Sweden's third largest city, in just thirty-five minutes. The two nations, which fought bitter wars in the past, are now holding hands.

Denmark enjoys an excellent telephone and telegraph system. Some 4.7 million regular telephones are in use, and one in every two Danes has a cellular telephone. More than half of the people regularly use the Internet. Avid readers, Danes are served by fifty daily newspapers. Just about all Danish households have at least one TV set. Danes watch many popular American and European TV shows. The Danish government sponsors two TV channels. One channel, Danmarks Radio

(DR), is commercial free; the other, TV2, allows limited commercials. The content of these two government-sponsored TV stations is the subject of lively debate in the press and in talk shows broadcast on the stations themselves.

Denmark and the Automobile

The Danes' devotion to clean air is almost legendary. The private automobile is the country's biggest polluter. Yet the car is a convenient method of transportation. Danes, like most other people, enjoy driving. Few Danes seriously suggest that their country should prohibit automobile use. But to discourage a dependence on automobiles, Danish leaders have made driving cars a very expensive form of transportation. Danes have to pay a whopping 200 percent tax every time they buy a new or used automobile. These taxes mean a midsize car worth $30,000 in the United States costs $90,000 in Denmark. Add to these expenses high prices for license plates and insurance. Gasoline hovers above $4 a gallon.

Even the simple routine of a young person's applying for a driver's license is costly. In Denmark you must be eighteen to request a driving test. And you'd better bring the family bankbook with you to the testing office. Government fees that have to be paid for obtaining a first driver's license total about $1,500 in American money.

Unlike in the United States, a person can readily live and work in Denmark without owning a car. Trains and buses run to every tiny village. A state-of-the-art subway system opened in Copenhagen in 2002. Pedal power is another energy-saving method of transportation. The nation has more bicycles than people. On street corners stand bike racks with tangles of parked bicycles. Bicycle-only lanes run through the heart of cities. Denmark's mostly flat land allows for easy pedaling. Of course, bicycling in the winter winds can be an ordeal. But Danes practically grow up on bicycles, and they will pedal their two-wheelers even into the teeth of a blizzard.

Bicycles outnumber people in Denmark.

Despite high costs and the availability of the transportation alternatives, one in three Danes owns a car. As traffic jams attest, plenty of Danes prefer driving over mass transit.

Trade and the EU

Each year Denmark exports (sells to markets abroad) more goods than it imports (buys from foreign trading partners). By selling more than it buys, the country maintains a healthy balance of trade. Denmark exports machinery, meat and meat products, dairy products, fish, furniture, ships, and windmills. The kingdom imports raw materials, chemicals, grain, and consumer goods such as clothes. Denmark's prime trading partners are Germany, Sweden, France, the Netherlands, Norway, and the United States.

Since 1973 Denmark has been a member of the European Union (EU). The organization began as a group of European countries that agreed to cut trade restrictions among group members. By the year 2002 the EU had fifteen member nations—Austria, Belgium, Denmark, France, Finland, Germany, Greece, Ireland, Italy, Luxembourg, the Netherlands, Portugal, Spain, Sweden, and the United Kingdom. In recent years the EU has grown to become a sort of super-government with its own parliament. Danes enjoy the free-trade aspects of the EU, but they have had disagreements with some of its policies. There is an ongoing conflict between Denmark and the EU. While few Danes wish to give up membership in the EU, many others decry the EU's tendency to dictate internal policies to its member nations.

California Windmills

Drive in rural California and you will see vast "windmill farms"— hundreds of whirling windmills that look like huge aircraft propellers. Many of those windmills are made in Denmark and exported to the United States.

On January 1, 1999, a new currency, the euro, was introduced to all member nations of the EU. A year later Danish citizens

In 2000, Danes voted down the use of the euro as their unit of currency.

voted to turn down the euro and continue using the country's old money, the *krone*. The country's preference for the old coins is another example of the Danes' desire for self-rule and independence from the EU. Many experts believe the people cling to their old money because the 10-krone coin has a picture of Queen Margrethe II on its face. If true, the voters' rejection of the euro proves once again that in Denmark the queen remains a very special person.

The Danish people will vote again as to whether they should accept the euro as their currency. Adopting the euro is not a requirement for EU membership. In 2002 Great Britain, Sweden, and Denmark continued to use their old currencies. But the euro looms as a tempting system of money because it is now in use by 304 million Europeans. The French gave up their cherished franc and the Germans their mark to use the euro. Can the Danes be far behind?

Visit Denmark, exchange your money at a bank, and hit the streets preparing to shop till you drop. Watch out! Danish prices

A Look at Danish Money

The kingdom's currency is based on the Danish krone (DK). In the year 2002 the DK exchanged at about 8 DK to U.S.$1. This means that if you bought a candy bar at a Danish store for 8 krone, its cost would be $1 in American money. The precise exchange rate (dollar to krone) varies from day to day.

Common bills are the 50, 100, 200, 500, and 1,000 DK notes. The notes bear the portraits of people who have made contributions to Danish art and culture. For example, the 50 DK note has a picture of the famous Danish-born writer Karen Blixen (Isak Dinesen). Coins come in 25 and 50 øre (an øre is the Danish equivalent to an American penny), 1 DK, 2 DK, 5 DK, 10 DK, and 20 DK. All coins are round, and the 1, 2, and 5 DK coins have holes in the middle.

are steep. Consider a purchase everyone understands—a McDonald's lunch. In Denmark in 2002, a Big Mac, fries, and a soft drink cost, in American money, $5.40. The same McDonald's meal in, say, Atlanta, Georgia, would run about $4.00.

Denmark is an expensive country. Taxes are one of the reasons for the steep prices. Each purchase at a restaurant or a shop carries a value-added tax of 25 percent. High prices for goods tend to be the rule in northern Europe. In fact, Denmark is said to be the cheapest of the three Scandinavian countries. There are ways that family vacationers get around the shocking costs. For example, camping in the rural areas saves money over hotel rates. Car rental is expensive, so families take the train or ride bicycles. Despite the high costs a vacation in Denmark is always an enjoyable experience.

Expensive Real Estate

Between 1995 and 2000 the cost of a house or a condominium apartment in central Copenhagen more than doubled.

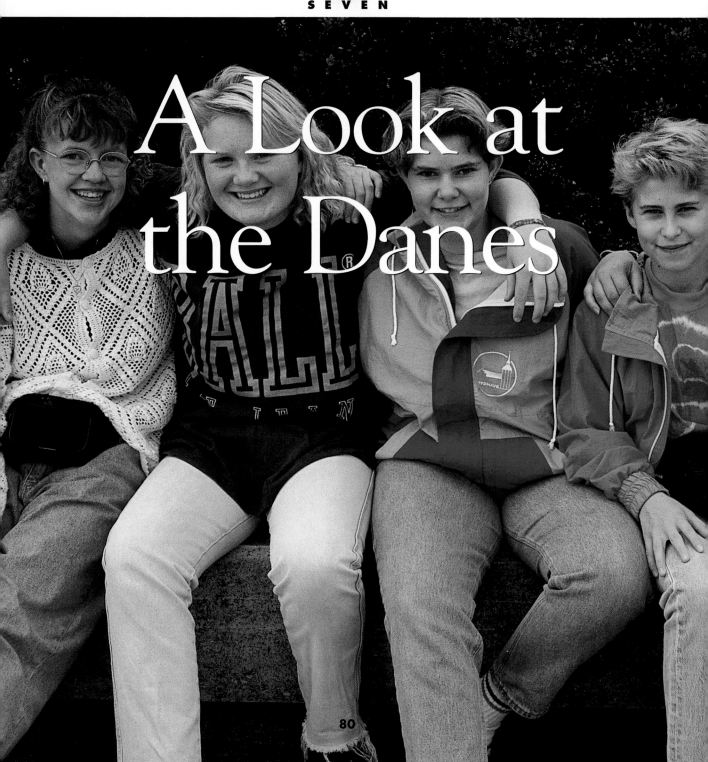

A Look at the Danes

THE AMERICAN HUMORIST GARRISON KEILLOR LIVED many years in Denmark and claims to speak the language "well enough to get into trouble but not well enough to get out of it." Keillor tells this story of typical Danish behavior: "People stand on the curb and wait for the red light to change, even if it's 2 A.M. and there's not a car in sight. The red light is part of the system: You cross against it, and you are showing disdain for your countrymen." Obedience to the red light serves as another example of the Danish belief that the country is a large family in which no one is special and everyone must abide by the rules.

Opposite: **Danish teens enjoy a field trip to Copenhagen.**

Population and People

The official census published in 1999 counted 5,313,577 people living in Denmark. Denmark's first official census was taken in 1769, and the population then was 798,000. More than 70 percent of the people live in cities and towns. Denmark is the smallest country in northern Europe, but it is

Denmark is one of the most populous countries in Europe.

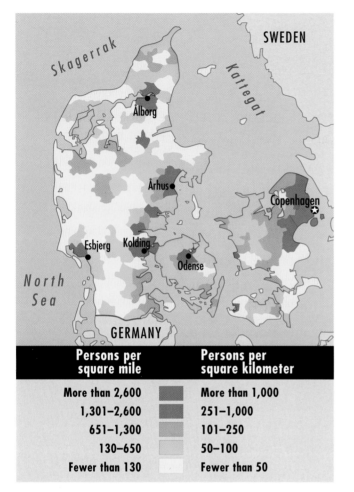

Persons per square mile		Persons per square kilometer
More than 2,600		More than 1,000
1,301–2,600		251–1,000
651–1,300		101–250
130–650		50–100
Fewer than 130		Fewer than 50

The Population of Denmark's Major Cities

Copenhagen	1.4 million
Århus	280,000
Odense	184,000
Ålborg	155,000
Esbjerg	73,000

the most densely populated. The kingdom holds 291 people per square mile, which makes it crowded compared with neighboring Sweden with 46 people per square mile.

About 95 percent of Danes are ethnic Scandinavians with deep roots in Denmark. The image of a Scandinavian person is that of a tall, slender blond with blue eyes. The image is only partially true. There are plenty of dark-skinned, black-haired Danes of Scandinavian background. However, blond hair is common, especially among children. Another popular belief about the "Danish look" is that the country's women possess striking beauty. Many world travelers agree that this belief is largely true.

Travel in rural Denmark and you are likely to see a stout grandmother-type pushing a heavy wheelbarrel as she works her farm. This picture suggests two aspects of the Danish people: (1) they are active in old age, and (2) they are an older population. About 15 percent of the population is older than sixty-five, while only 21 percent are younger than seventeen years of age. In the near future there will be relatively few people of childbearing age, and it is believed the Danish

The Danish population has a large sector of active seniors.

population will fall below 5 million. This situation will put a strain on Danish welfare because there will be fewer working-age men and women who will contribute to the system and more older folks who will collect pensions.

Ethnic make up of Denmark

Today, fewer than 5 percent of Danish residents are foreign-born. The number of newcomers in Denmark has doubled during the past twenty years. Each ethnic group in Denmark makes up less than 1 percent of the total population. Ranked from the largest group to the smallest, the Danes can be classified as follows: Scandinavians, Inuit Eskimo (from

"Hi There, Sen"

Up until the mid-1800s Danish common people did not use last names. Instead, the males added *sen* (meaning "son") to their father's first name. Thus Peter's son became Petersen. Today two out of every three Danes have names ending in *sen*. The most common names are Jensen, Nielsen, and Hansen.

Danish children and immigrant children from Africa enjoy a sunny day at the playground.

Greenland), Faroese (from the Faroe Islands), German, Turkish, Iranian, and Somalian. Many immigrants are Muslims from the Middle East or nonwhites from Asia and Africa. Danes regard themselves as a fair-minded people who dislike racism. Still, they worry that immigration is changing the character of their country and that the changes are coming too fast for many people to accept.

Road signs in Danish point the way.

The Danish language is part of the northern Germanic language group. Swedes and Norwegians can, with some difficulty, communicate with Danes. Danish is a difficult language for the foreigner to grasp because it is not pronounced as it is spelled. Vowels often have different pronunciations. Whole syllables are sometimes swallowed by the speaker. Even the Royal Danish Embassy in Washington, D.C., admits that the language sounds rather quirky to the visitor: "Many people say that Danes speak as if they have a hot potato in their mouths."

Having no knowledge of Danish will not hinder a traveler from North America. In Danish schools all students

A Brief Lesson in Danish

The Danish language uses the same twenty-six letters as English does, but the Danes add three letters to their alphabet: ø (which is pronounced like the "u" in "nurse"), æ (like the "e" in "egg"), and å (like the "a" in "paw"). Here are some common expressions useful when traveling in Denmark:

Goddag	Hello (good day)
Farvel	Goodbye (farewell)
Va or jo	Yes
Nej	No
Tak	Thank you
Gade	Road
Værelser	Rooms
Kød	Meat
Penge	Money
Cykle	Ride a bicycle

begin studying English at age ten. High school students take courses in both English and German. Speaking either English or German, a vacationer can go anywhere in Denmark with no great problem.

People attempting to speak Danish should not be afraid of making a mistake and then being laughed at because of the blunder. Danes enjoy talking to outsiders who try to master their somewhat complicated language. Above all, Danes like people with good manners. So if you try to speak Danish and get hopelessly confused, simply say *tak* ("thank you").

Danish-Americans

Danes have been in the United States since its beginnings as a nation. One of George Washington's finest officers was Hans Christian Febiger, affectionately dubbed Old Denmark by his men. In the 1800s more than 300,000 Danish immigrants arrived on American shores. States such as Minnesota, Wisconsin, and Iowa had farming villages made up entirely of Danish immigrants. Here are just a few notable Danish-Americans:

Peter Lassen (1800–1859): A Danish-born blacksmith, Lassen led a group of settlers west over the Rocky Mountains and blazed a trail later used by California gold prospectors; California's Lassen Volcanic National Park is named in his honor.

Jacob August Riis (1849–1914): Born in Ribe, Denmark, Riis came to the United States at age twenty-one and became a photographer with a social conscience; powerful photographs in his book *How the Other Half Lives* (1890) alerted American citizens to the plight of poor people living in city slums.

The Danes' Gifts to English

Ages ago Viking invaders from Denmark put their own stamp on the English language. The god Wdin (also pronounced "Odin") was honored in the middle of the week (Wdin's Day), which became "Wednesday" in English. Odin's son, Thor, had his special day on Thursday, or Thor's Day.

Gutzon Borglum (1867–1941): Borglum was born to a Danish immigrant family in Idaho and became a gifted sculptor; in 1927 he started his most grandiose work—Mount Rushmore in South Dakota—where he carved the faces of four American presidents into a cliff face—those of George Washington, Thomas Jefferson, Theodore Roosevelt, and Abraham Lincoln.

Victor Borge (1909–2000): Borge performed comic routines while playing classical music on the piano; in the late 1930s he directed his musical jokes against Adolf Hitler and was forced to flee Denmark to the United States, where he became a famous entertainer.

Born to Danish parents, Gutzon Borglum went on to sculpt Mount Rushmore in the Black Hills of South Dakota.

A People and Their Church

Too much pomp and striving will bring us no rest.
Keeping our feet firmly on the ground is best.
—N.F.S. Grundtvig, Danish philosopher and theologian

SURVEYS SHOW THAT AN OVERWHELMING NUMBER OF Danes believe in God. But only 3 percent of Danish men and women say they go to church more than twice a month. Most of the regular churchgoers are elderly people. About half of the Danish public attends church for special occasions such as Christmas or Easter.

Denmark has a state religion, the Evangelical Lutheran Church, which grew out of the Reformation in the early

Opposite: **Most Danes attend church only on holidays. Regular churchgoers are primarily the elderly.**

Saint Albans, the "English church," in Copenhagen

1500s. Nine out of ten Danes claim membership in this state church even though they might or might not attend services. Danes enjoy complete freedom of religion. Mosques, synagogues, and Catholic churches are established throughout the land.

Just about all Danish young people grow up in contact with their church. For a baby's baptism, family members gather at their local church, where the minister blesses the newborn. At age fourteen most Danes are confirmed into a life of Christianity. Confirmation is the occasion for a party where family friends attend and shower the young person with gifts.

Another holiday celebrated by the young illustrates Denmark's shift from strict religious practices to simply having fun. Today, *Festelavn* is a Danish version of trick-or-treat.

Children celebrating Festelavn, the Danish tradition of trick-or-treating

Years ago the holiday called for all Danish Lutherans to fast (to go without food). The opposite is now true. At Festelavn, celebrated in late February, kids dress up in costumes and go to school. The ones with the most outrageous costumes are elected king and queen of the festival. After school children go door to door collecting candy or coins in tin cups. The evening ends as the kids gorge themselves with sweets. And to think this holiday began ages ago as a day of religious fasting!

Religion as a Philosophy

While Danes may shun church services, they practice a Christian way of life as a day-to-day habit. They reject violence, and they protect citizens from hunger and homelessness. To the Danes these Christian practices stem as much from philosophy as from commandments written in the Bible. Perhaps this philosophy is rooted in the religious thinking of two historic Danes.

Refuge for a God

A legend says that when the Danes became Christians hundreds of years ago, their most powerful god, Odin, withdrew to the Danish island of Møn and hid among its enchanting white cliffs. Some storytellers claim that the disappointed god is still there, weeping and feeling betrayed by humankind.

Nikolai Frederik Severin Grundtvig was born in 1783 to a religious family. In his youth he rebelled against the dictatorial bishops who ran his church. N.F.S. Grundtvig advocated a democratic church, one whose leaders had faith in the wisdom of their parishioners. A man of enormous energy, he dabbled in politics, becoming a member of parliament. He also wrote the words for many hymns. Today all Danes sing his hymns during the Christmas season. N.F.S. Grundtvig died in 1872 when he was almost ninety. While little known outside of Denmark, Grundtvig's work influenced the modern kingdom more than that of any other Dane.

When studying the Bible as a boy, the Danish philosopher Søren Aabye Kierkegaard (1813–1855) became fascinated with the story of Abraham. Why, Kierkegaard wondered, did God command Abraham to kill his only son, Isaac? He concluded that God was testing Abraham's faith, and when Abraham responded in the correct manner, he became a "knight of faith." Kierkegaard lived most of his life in Copenhagen and continued wrestling with questions of morality and religion. His books are read by students throughout the world to this day. Some non-Danes learn Danish primarily to be able to read Kierkegaard in his original language. Many scholars claim that the Danish religious thinker laid the groundwork for a philosophy called existentialism.

Denmark's Round Churches

Denmark has few grandiose and ornamental churches. Its churches were built largely by local people and designed to fit the modest needs of the community. Some of those churches were built in an age when warfare was more or less constant. At Østerlars on the island of Bornholm rises the *Rundkirke* (round church) (below). Dating from 1150, this circular building has thick walls designed to withstand missiles hurled by an attacking enemy. Three other churches on Bornholm also have fortresslike round designs.

Arts, Entertainment, and Culture

94

Danes are a hardworking people, but even the most diligent worker deserves a day off. Danes fill their off hours with sports, the movies, reading, and pursuing the arts.

Opposite: **Danes enjoy a day of leisure at Tivoli Gardens.**

The Sporting Life

Ask a group of Danes to name their favorite sport, and the answer will come in a chorus: *fodbold* (football). The game that Americans call soccer is played in grade schools, in high schools, and in fields in every tiny village. Football is easily

Denmark's most popular sport, football (soccer), is played by children as well as adults.

The Football Family

Two of Denmark's top football players were brothers Michael (below) and Brian Laudrup. Neither brother plays professional soccer anymore, but they both are living legends in the sport. Michael (born in 1964) passed the ball with astonishing accuracy, and Brian (born in 1969) was such a superb dribbler that it seemed he had an invisible string attached from his foot to the ball. It is no wonder these two were such accomplished football players. Their father, Finn Laudrup (born in 1945), was an all-Denmark player from 1967 through 1979.

Denmark's most passionately followed spectator sport. The entire kingdom celebrated in 1992 when the Danish national team beat its archrival Germany 2–0 to capture the European championship. In 1998 the national team made the quarterfinals in the World Cup, the greatest soccer competition of all.

Aside from soccer, Danes are avid basketball, tennis, and badminton players. More than 3 million people belong to various sporting organizations such as football clubs, gymnastic clubs, and rifle-shooting clubs. There are about 1,000 badminton courts in Denmark. Golf is the country's fastest-

Danes enjoy a friendly game of basketball.

The Danish National Cycling Routes

Everyone rides in this country, where there are more bicycles than people. Denmark has ten recognized cycling routes that together run more than 3,000 miles and take riders through marvelous country scenery.

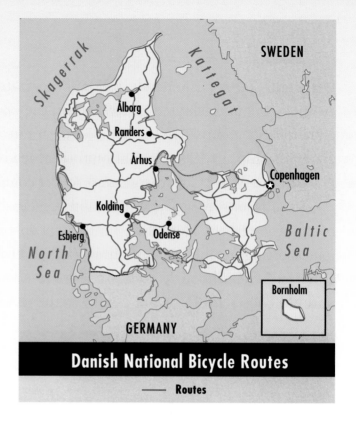

Danish National Bicycle Routes

—— Routes

growing sport. Hiking is a weekend activity for families and members of hiking clubs.

In schools, girls' sports are treated on an equal level with sports for boys. Still, boys and girls develop different preferences. Danish boys play football, handball, and badminton. Girls pursue gymnastics, badminton, horseback riding, hand-

Sportsman of the Century

The Danes love for the sea is illustrated in their success in the sport of yachting. Denmark's greatest yachtsman is Paul Elvstrøm (born 1928). Elvstrøm competed in nine Olympic Games and won four gold medals.

A designer as well as a sailor, he fashioned his own sails and built yachts from the keel up. In 1996 Paul Elvstrøm was chosen the Danish Sportsman of the Century.

ball, and swimming. The nation cheered the Danish women's handball team that won gold medals at the summer Olympic Games in 1996 and 2000.

Denmark's Tonje Kjaergaard (in red) during the World Handball Championship in 1999

The Arts

The early 1800s is a period often called the Golden Age of Danish art. One prominent artist of the time was the sculptor Bertel Thorvaldsen (1770–1844). Thorvaldsen re-created the classical statues of Rome, and in 1836 he founded the

Romanesque statues at the Thorvaldsen Art Museum in Copenhagen

Thorvaldsen Art Museum, which can be visited today in Copenhagen. Kristoffer Vilhelm Eckersberg (1783–1853), sometimes described as the Father of Danish Art, was the leading Golden Age painter. Eckersberg's scenes of everyday Danish life in the nineteenth century are admired for their marvelous attention to detail.

More than 100 years ago painters from Denmark and Sweden came to the Danish island of Bornholm, a haven for the arts, to spend the summer. The artists were attracted by sunlight glittering over the island's beaches. Today the island remains a lively center for silversmiths, jewelers, and craftspeople. Vacationers are invited into Bornholm's small shops to watch the craftspersons at work and pick out items to buy.

A potter turns a clay pot in his Bornholm studio.

A Danish modern-art movement was led by a multiple-nation group known as Cobra (so called because the group had members from Copenhagen, Brussels, and Amsterdam). The Cobra organization was founded by Asger Jorn (1914–1973) who was both a painter and an engraver. Per Kirkeby (born 1938) creates large and often comical sculptures for public

parks and squares. Lovers of contemporary paintings flock to the Louisiana Museum of Modern Art in the north Zealand town of Humlebæk. Opened in 1958, the museum features a children's section and an exciting sculpture garden. More than a half-million people visit the museum each year. Another "artsy" community is the seaside town of Skagen in northern Jutland. In the 1870s Skagen artists such as Michael and Anna Archer and P. S. Krfyer painted brilliant beach scenes that are now highly valued abroad.

Danish Design

A kitchen chair should be more than just a place to sit. A table should be something other than a surface upon which to put a plate. So say artists of the school of Danish design. Just after World War II a group of Danes turned their attention to everyday furniture and transformed common pieces into objects of art. The movement began in 1949 when architect Karre Klint (1888–1954) created the Round Chair, a chair that fitted a seated person almost like a baseball glove fits a ball. This revolutionary furniture became known as Danish modern, and people everywhere furnished their entire houses with the new designs. Danish modern creations range from far-out-looking lamps and coffeepots to down-to-earth, practical furniture. One brainchild of Danish modern is The Ant, the interlocking stacking chairs designed by Arne Jacobson now found in meeting halls throughout the world. Danish modern housewares are on display at two Copenhagen museums—the Danish Museum of Decorative Art and the Danish Design Center.

Denmark is a nation of readers. Each year 12,000 books are published in the kingdom. Danes borrow more library books per capita (about 109 million books a year) than any other people on earth. Given these impressive statistics, it is not surprising that tiny Denmark has produced so many great writers.

Hans Christian Andersen (1805–1875) is Denmark's most famous author. His fairy tales are read by adults as well as by children. The stories often have hidden meanings and are told

Borrowing more than 100 million books a year from the library, Danes of all ages enjoy a good book.

Hamlet's Castle

Kronborg Castle was built in the 1400s in the town of Helsingør, which is north of Copenhagen. Many people claim it is the most beautiful castle in northern Europe. It is also a place of legends. In the castle cellar, so one legend goes, rests the Viking chief Holger Danske, who will rise from his sleep and go to war if Denmark is ever attacked. Kronborg has a literary legend too. In 1602 the great English playwright William Shakespeare used the castle as a background for his tragic play *Hamlet*. The play features a legendary Danish prince, Hamlet, who grieves over his dead father and ponders suicide himself as he utters the famous line "To be, or not to be—that is the question."

Hans Christian Andersen, author of classic fairy tales such as "The Ugly Duckling"

with sly humor. Born in the city of Odense to an impoverished family, Andersen moved to Copenhagen when he was fourteen. He almost starved as he attempted to make a living as a singer and an actor. Andersen finally earned money as a writer of plays, but those dramas are rarely performed these days. The writer became world renowned with fanciful stories such as "The Ugly Duckling," "The Little Mermaid," and "The Emperor's New Clothes." In all, he published 156 stories, many of them classics that have been enjoyed by generations of readers. Andersen fell in love with at least three women, but he never married. His life was devoted to his art, and he is now hailed as one of the greatest storytellers of all time.

Karen Blixen (1885–1962) was born in Rungsted to a wealthy family. Writing under the pen name Isak Dinesen, she published supernatural stories that were based on old legends. Her volumes of short stories, *Seven Gothic Tales* (1934) and *Winter's Tales* (1942), were widely read in the English-speaking world because Blixen wrote in both Danish and English. Blixen lived for fifteen years in Kenya, and her memoir, *Out of Africa* (1937), is her most famous work.

Peter Høeg (born 1957) is Denmark's leading modern writer. In 1992 he published *Miss Smilla's Feeling for Snow*, a mystery novel that takes place in Copenhagen and Greenland. The novel became a worldwide best-seller and appeared in the United States under the title *Smilla's Sense of Snow*. In another novel, *The History of Danish Dreams*, Høeg portrays the lives of misfits—those who simply can't conform to the sometimes rigid rules of Danish society.

Carl Nielsen, Danish composer and conductor

The Musical Scene

Music is the heartbeat of Denmark. The people enjoy every beat and style—from rock to rap, from classical to jazz. A love of music has deep roots in the kingdom.

Carl Nielsen (1865–1931) was born on the island of Fyn near Odense. As a music student, Nielsen was influenced by the Austrian composer Wolfgang Amadeus Mozart and the German composer Johannes Brahms. He is best known for writing six symphonies and a comic opera, *Maskerade*. Nielsen conducted the Royal Opera in Copenhagen for many years. Today the Carl Nielsen Museum in Odense tells the story of his life and music.

The Danish Royal Ballet performs at the National Theater in Copenhagen.

Performers at the Danish Royal Ballet seem to defy the law of gravity as they sail through the air in graceful leaps. When the 150-year-old ballet company goes on its annual worldwide tours, people wonder how a nation of only 5 million people can produce so many outstanding dancers. The answer lies in the fact that all Danes are eager to participate in this cherished institution. Recently even Queen Margrethe II designed costumes for the dancers. The Danish Royal Ballet performs traditional works such as Tchaikovsky's *Swan Lake* and *The Nutcracker* as well as experimental pieces that have no storylines. Denmark is one of the few countries where a ballet dancer rises to the status of national hero. Copenhagen's Erik Bruhn (1928–1986) danced for the Danish Royal Ballet, and at his peak he was celebrated all over the kingdom as the greatest male dancer in the world.

The Olsen Brothers are living legends of pop and rock music. Jørgen and Niels "Noller" Olsen were born in Odense in the 1950s and moved to Copenhagen with their family when they were young. They began as a rock duo singing most of their songs in English. In the early 1970s the brothers were youth idols, and their posters were pinned to the bedroom walls of teenage girls. Remarkably their popularity with the young has

Denmark's Woodstock

In 1969 bearded and beaded American hippies gathered in a farmer's field in Woodstock, New York, and held a grand rock festival and love-in. Not to be outdone, Denmark put on its own rock blast in 1971 at the town of Roskilde, Zealand. The musicfest became an annual event. About 90,000 young people from Germany, Scandinavia, and other parts of Europe flock to Roskilde each summer to enjoy four days of nonstop music. Over the years famous performers such as Bob Dylan and the band U2 have entertained revelers at Roskilde.

endured. To this day high-schoolers cherish their posters, although the brothers now have gray hair. In 2000 the Olsen Brothers won the European Song Festival with their lively song "Fly on the Wings of Love."

Danish cities and towns host more than 175 music festivals each year. The Copenhagen Jazz Festival, held in July, is a ten-day long musical event that brings some of the world's best jazz groups to the capital. Also in July, the cities of Århus and Maribo hold jazz extravaganzas. The Danish version of country music is the theme for the Scandinavian Country Club's Country Music Festival held in August at Silkeborg.

Theater and Film

The greatest name in Danish theater is also its oldest. The playwright Ludvig Holberg (1684–1754) wrote works featuring comic characters such as a barber who talks too much and a soldier who is given to bragging. Holberg's plays, which include *The Political Thinker* and *Jeppe of the Hill*, are performed in Copenhagen and in small theaters throughout Denmark. Holberg was also a historian, and his *History of the Danish Kingdoms* is still read by scholars.

Nikoline Werdelin (born 1960) is a modern playwright who got her start drawing cartoons in Danish newspapers. Her comic strip "Cafe," which took place in a small restaurant, was widely read. In the 1990s Werdelin's play *The Blind Painter* became a hit with Danish audiences.

Some Danish theater groups cater to the young. More than 100 children's theater companies regularly tour the country and put on plays especially aimed at kids. Puppet theater leaves small children giggling in delight.

Danes are justly proud of their film industry. Each year Danish companies produce ten to sixteen feature films. The Danes' love for cinema goes back many decades. Carl Theodor Dreyer (1889–1968) produced the black-and-white masterpiece *The Passion of Joan of Arc* in 1928, and the movie remains a treasure among film historians. In more recent times the Danish films *Babette's Feast* (1986), which is based on a story by Karen Blixen, and *Pelle the Conqueror* (1987) won Academy Awards in Hollywood for the best foreign film of the year. The Danish-made film *Dancer in the Dark* won the European Film Academy Award for Best Movie in the year 2000.

Danes are world famous for creating a special type of film called Dogme 95. Such films feature no artificial light or sound. A movie called *The Celebration* was the first Dogme 95 film. Today many American moviemakers study this Danish technique.

Danes of Science

Niels Bohr (1885–1962), born in Copenhagen, was the first scientist to accurately describe how atoms emit radiation. In

1922 Bohr won the Nobel Prize for physics for his work on atomic structure. During World War II, Bohr escaped German-occupied Denmark and traveled to the United States, where he helped American scientists build the first atomic bomb. Bohr later became a spokesman for the peaceful uses of atomic energy. His son, Aage Niels Bohr, won a Nobel Prize for physics in 1975.

Danish researchers and doctors have had a long history of advancing the cause of medicine. Thomas Bartholin (1616–1680) discovered the lymphatic system, which returns fluid from body tissues to the bloodstream. Niels Finsen (1860–1904) was the first doctor to use infrared light to cure skin diseases. Johannes Fibiger (1867–1928) determined that cancer can be caused by exposure to such pollutants as tar. Carl Peter Henrik Dam (1895–1976) won the Nobel Prize for his discovery of vitamin K.

Nobel Prizes

Nobel Prizes are awarded each year by the Royal Academy of Sciences in Stockholm, Sweden. A panel of experts presents the awards to people who have made outstanding achievements in six fields—physics, chemistry medicine, literature, peace, and economics. Between 1901 (when the awards were first presented) and 2001 Danes have won thirteen of the treasured prizes.

Everyday Life

C H A P T E R

T E N

112

D AWN BREAKS IN DENMARK. MEN AND WOMEN GO TO work. Children go to school. Everyone has something to do. The people's day-to-day routine—their work and their play— can reveal much about Danish society.

Opposite: **Going to school daily is a must for all children in Denmark.**

Living the Good Life—Well, Sort Of

A wealthy Danish man recently sold his Mercedes-Benz automobile and bought a very ordinary-looking car. Why? He said he got tired of people pointing to his expensive car while he drove down the street. The lesson in this story is clear: If you are rich in Denmark, you don't show your wealth. Displays of wealth are considered to be bad manners, because in Denmark a rich man is no better than anyone else.

Although they shun "showy" riches, the Danes try to live as comfortably as they can. Much of a family's budget is

A typical home in Denmark

Flowers bloom in this well-cared-for garden.

assigned to its house. Fifty-five percent of Danish families own their own homes. In most other European countries a majority of the people rent. The common dwelling is a *parcelhus*, a small bungalow with a garden in the back. Often the garden is surrounded by a brick wall or hedges. Whether they are well-off or working class, Danes are superb gardeners. In every yard the bushes will be neatly trimmed and the fruit trees pruned. During the summer flowers bloom everywhere.

Small towns are a collection of bungalow-type houses with a downtown section in the center. Streets in the central section are lined with cafés and stores. Also in the middle of town are usually one or two churches, a movie house, and a city hall. Danish towns tend to be compact. People easily walk

Danish towns are small, allowing shoppers to walk from store to store.

to and from the stores, the library, school, and the doctor's office. The towns' outskirts end at farmers' fields. Unlike in the United States, towns in Denmark do not erode into a sea of suburban parking lots and shopping malls.

Clothing

For everyday use the Danes wear clothes identical to those worn elsewhere in Western Europe and in the United States. Danes are not known to be fancy dressers. Men who work in offices rarely are required to wear neckties. Women also wear casual clothes to work or when performing chores.

On festival days men and women may wear traditional country clothing of a type that was in fashion a hundred years ago. Many of these country pieces hang in museums today. In the old days flowing ankle-length dresses were made at home by women and worn proudly. Bonnets and scarfs were particularly important in women's costumes. A married woman with children wore a black bonnet to church to show her dignity. Young, unmarried women wore bright bonnets decorated with flowers. Men's traditional outfits featured knee breeches usually made from leather.

Dining Danish Style

Danes like hearty eating—perhaps they eat too well. Diet books have become top sellers, and gyms have opened so that people can work off extra pounds. Health matters are always a concern. The average life expectancy among Danes is seventy-two years for men and seventy-eight for women. This is

Eating a good meal is important to many Danes.

not a high longevity rate by European standards. Heart disease is the cause of death for 50 percent of the women and 58 percent of the men. Contributing to heart disease is the Danish love for fatty foods, sweets, beer, and smoking.

Breakfast is the lightest meal taken in Denmark. It usually consists of cereal and milk, bread, or a sweet roll accompanied by coffee or tea. Huge American breakfasts such as bacon and eggs are not the rule. In fact, the bigger restaurants in Danish cities do not even open until around noon.

Lunch is a good occasion to feast in an honored Danish tradition: eating open-faced sandwiches called *smørrebrød*. Restaurants make the sandwiches fresh daily and display them in their windows. Smørrebrød can be made with fish, meat, eggs, or salads. One normally eats smørrebrød with a knife and fork. The special sandwiches allow a person to savor good Danish bread. Rye bread is the common fare. Danish rye is dense and packed with seeds and can serve as a meal on its own.

Traditional open-faced sandwiches, or smørrebrød

A Recipe for Æblepandekager (Danish Apple Pancakes)

This dish is more like a cake than like traditional pancakes. No matter, Ælepandekager is a sinfully delicious treat.

6 eggs
1/2 cup milk
1 cup sugar
1 cup flour
1/2 teaspoon salt
1/2 cup cream
3 apples, peeled and sliced
Butter
Cinnamon
Juice from one lemon

Beat eggs lightly, and add milk. Combine sugar, flour, and salt; add to egg mixture. Stir in cream. Fry apple slices over medium-high heat in butter until they are golden brown. Cover the bottom of a lightly buttered baking dish with the fried apples. Pour the batter made from the eggs and other ingredients over the apples. Bake at 500°F for 20 to 25 minutes. Sprinkle cinnamon and lemon juice over the top. Return to oven and bake an additional 10 minutes. Serves 6.

Coffee and a....

In the United States a sweet roll is called a Danish, as in "Let's have coffee and a Danish." In Denmark that same sweet roll is a *wienerbrød*, or "Vienna bread."

Danish dinners differ little from suppertime dishes served in the United States. Fish or meat is the main course. Some cooks like to make spicy Danish meatballs and serve them on a bed of cooked cabbage. Adults may drink a glass of wine with their dinner. A nut-filled coffee cake called *kringel* is a favorite dessert.

Education

Getting an education fills daily life for Danish young people. Laws require that all children attend school from first through

ninth grades. After the ninth grade (usually reached at age six-teen) about half of the young people seek jobs, while another half go on to high school or to vocational schools. Danish high schools (called gymnasiums) are demanding. Exams are held weekly, and homework is frequent. The pace of study heats up before the final exam, which high-schoolers must pass in order to graduate. High-school graduation is the occasion for student parties that sometimes last for several days.

Danish grade schools tend to have a relaxed atmosphere. Kids commonly refer to their teacher by his or her first name. No school requires students to wear uniforms, even though

A grade-school classroom has a relaxed atmosphere where students can even call their teacher by his or her first name!

school uniforms are common in other European countries. All schools are coed, admitting both girls and boys. Summer vacation for grade schools begins around June 20 and ends near August 10.

After three years of high school a young Dane is eligible for college. Major universities are in Copenhagen, Odense, and Ålborg. The oldest and largest of the three is the University of Copenhagen (founded in 1479), which has about 24,000 students. A college education is free for all students who qualify.

A Special Teacher for Special Students

Dr. Lilli Nielsen was born on the island of Bornholm in 1926. Three of her brothers and sisters were blind. As a special-education teacher, she pioneered a system called active learning, which surrounds blind children with interesting objects to touch. This method inspires the children to learn. Today she travels throughout the world teaching her system. Dr. Nielsen taught for thirty years at the Royal Institute for the Blind in Copenhagen. In 1996 she received the ultimate honor for Danish citizens when she was knighted by Queen Margrethe II.

The Folk Schools

Denmark is world famous for its unique brand of adult education called the folk schools. The folk-school movement grew out of the farm cooperatives that were formed in the early 1800s. Within the cooperatives were informal schools, paid for by the government, that allowed farmers to improve their reading and writing skills. The spiritual father of these schools was the theologian and hymn writer N.F.S. Grundtvig. Today the kingdom has about twenty major folk schools. Men and women attend the schools simply for the love of learning. No formal diplomas are awarded. The schools sponsor dances and discussion groups as well as holding classes.

Holidays and Festivals

Hygge is that wonderfully Danish word that means the light-hearted feeling one gets when having fun with family and friends. This special term, hygge, is heard often during holidays and festive occasions.

April Fools' Day lets Danes express their zany brand of humor. On the first of April do not be alarmed if a radio announcer claims that the United States and Denmark just declared war against each other; the announcer will soon say, "April fool!"

At midnight on New Year's Eve, Danes watch the queen give an annual address on TV. After the speech people at home stand and join the queen in singing the Danish national anthem.

It is an old tradition to hold a party for what Danes call a person's "round birthday." One's round birthday marks the end of his or her decade—ten, twenty, forty, and so forth. A round-birthday party is usually a family affair with only relatives and a few close friends invited. The round-birthday festivals are most important when grandmothers or grandfathers reach their seventies and eighties.

On the evening of June 23 city people travel to the countryside, gather up sticks and branches, and build bonfires. As they watch the blaze, men and women join in song. The bonfire tradition marks Midsummer Day and is based on ancient religious practices. Sometimes the effigy of a witch is tossed into the flames. An old tradition says burning the figure of a witch on Midsummer Day chases away evil spirits for the rest of the year.

National Holidays

Schools and banks close on those days recognized as national holidays by the Danish government. Those holidays are:

New Year's Day	January
Maundy Thursday (the Thursday before Easter)	March or April
Good Friday (the Friday before Easter)	March or April
Easter Sunday	March or April
Easter Monday	March or April
Common Prayer Day (fourth Friday after Easter)	April or May
Ascension Day (fifth Thursday after Easter)	May or June
Whitsunday (seventh Sunday after Easter)	May or June
Whitmonday (eighth Monday after Easter)	May or June
Constitution Day	June
Christmas Eve	December
Christmas Day	December
Boxing Day	December

Tivoli, Denmark's Garden of Fun

One of Europe's oldest amusement parks, Copenhagen's Tivoli Gardens opened in 1843. It is small, only 20 acres (8 ha) by U.S. amusement-park standards, and the rides are not anywhere nearly as wild. A rickety wooden roller coaster dating from 1914 is as high a ride as the park offers. A nearby ferris wheel looks like a museum piece. But its beauty and its antiquity make this park a must visit. During the summer months some 400,000 flowers bloom at Tivoli. Walk at night under the 110,000 lanterns and you will hear music coming at you from every direction. Fireworks displays are nightly events. Tivoli Gardens is a part of the Danish soul. In all, 4 million people, two-thirds of whom are Danish citizens, visit the park each year. Don't expect anything Disney-like here, although Walt Disney was inspired by Tivoli when he built his first theme park, Disneyland, in California. Tivoli is a Danish institution, and the people like it that way.

A grand party is held at Denmark's only national park once a year to celebrate—of all things—American independence. Every Fourth of July thousands of people gather at

Rebild Bakker Park is where Danes celebrate the United States' day of independence, July 4.

Rebild Bakker Park, near Ålborg, where they hold square dances, eat hot dogs, and listen to speeches by prominent Americans. President Ronald Reagan spoke there on one occasion. The Independence Day party reminds both countries of the masses of Danes that have immigrated to the United States. The festival also recalls that Rebild Bakker Park was purchased in 1912 by a group of Danish-Americans and given to the kingdom for use as parkland.

Events held in the kingdom are as varied as the Danish imagination. In May the city of Ribe holds a Viking Market complete with costumed actors and demonstrations of archery. The Round Zealand boat race challenges yacht teams from all over Europe to race around the island of Zealand for fun and prizes. Medieval jousters gather every July in the town of Åbenrå for the annual Tilting Festival. Kids love the Kite Flying Festival held on the island of Rømø every September.

Farvel Means Goodby in Danish

The first grand sight most tourists to Denmark behold is the statue of the Little Mermaid on the Copenhagen waterfront. It is also a proper spot to say *farvel* to the Kingdom of Denmark. The Little Mermaid sits beside the sea that is always present in the tiny kingdom. She waits, with angelic patience, for her lover to return. Denmark waits, too, for visitors to come once again. All people who visit this lovely nation long to return.

Timeline

Danish History		World History
Nomadic hunters settle permanently in what is now Denmark.	10,000 B.C.E.	
The people of Denmark and the rest of Europe learn how to grow crops and domesticate animals.	3000 B.C.E.	
		2500 B.C. Egyptians build the Pyramids and the Sphinx in Giza.
		563 B.C. The Buddha is born in India.
		A.D. 313 The Roman emperor Constantine recognizes Christianity.
A tribe called the Danes migrate to Denmark from Sweden and bring with them the language used in Denmark today.	500 A.D.	
		610 The Prophet Muhammad begins preaching a new religion called Islam.
The first recorded Viking raid on English soil takes place as Danish Norsemen attack a village in Dorset, England.	789	
Sweyn Forkbeard crowns himself king of Denmark and England.	1013	
Danish rule over England ends, and the Viking Age comes to a close.	1042	
		1054 The Eastern (Orthodox) and Western (Roman) Churches break apart.
		1066 William the Conqueror defeats the English in the Battle of Hastings.
		1095 Pope Urban II proclaims the First Crusade.
The city of Copenhagen is officially founded by Bishop Absalon.	1167	
		1215 King John seals the Magna Carta.
		1300s The Renaissance begins in Italy.
		1347 The Black Death sweeps through Europe.
Queen Margrethe I takes the throne.	1375	
Denmark, Sweden, and Norway unite in the Union of Kalmar.	1397	
		1453 Ottoman Turks capture Constantinople, conquering the Byzantine Empire.
		1492 Columbus arrives in North America.
		1500s The Reformation leads to the birth of Protestantism.
Ten-year-old Christian IV becomes king and rules Denmark for the next sixty years; Denmark makes great progress during his reign.	1588	
A set of laws called the Royal Act gives the king of Denmark broad powers.	1665	

Danish History

During the Napoleonic Wars, British fleets sail into Copenhagen harbor and bombard the city with cannon fire.	**1801 and 1807**
Norway separates from the Danish kingdom and becomes a part of Sweden.	1814
A new constitution establishes a Danish parliament with two houses and ends the absolute power of the monarchy.	1849
World War I begins in Europe; Denmark remains neutral throughout the conflict.	1914
World War II begins; once more the Danes declare neutrality, but German armies invade in April 1940, and for five years Denmark is occupied by the Germans.	1939
Iceland breaks away from Denmark and becomes an independent country.	1944
Danish voters approve a new constitution that establishes a one-house parliament and ends the "kings only" rule in the monarchy.	1953
Queen Margrethe II takes the throne on January 15.	1972
Denmark joins the organization that becomes the European Union (EU).	1973
Danish voters reject the euro and choose to keep their old currency, the Danish krone.	2000
In an election marked by heated arguments over immigration, the people choose a conservative government whose leaders vow to reduce the numbers of foreign workers coming to Denmark.	2001

World History

1776	The Declaration of Independence is signed.
1789	The French Revolution begins.
1865	The American Civil War ends.
1914	World War I breaks out.
1917	The Bolshevik Revolution brings communism to Russia.
1929	Worldwide economic depression begins.
1939	World War II begins, following the German invasion of Poland.
1945	World War II ends.
1957	The Vietnam War starts.
1969	Humans land on the moon.
1975	The Vietnam War ends.
1979	Soviet Union invades Afghanistan.
1983	Drought and famine in Africa.
1989	The Berlin Wall is torn down, as communism crumbles in Eastern Europe.
1991	Soviet Union breaks into separate states.
1992	Bill Clinton is elected U.S. president.
2000	George W. Bush is elected U.S. president.
2001	Terrorists attack World Trade Center towers, New York, and Pentagon, Washington, D.C.

Fast Facts

Official name: Kingdom of Denmark (*Kongeriget Danmark*)

Capital: Copenhagen (*København*)

Official language: Danish

Copenhagen

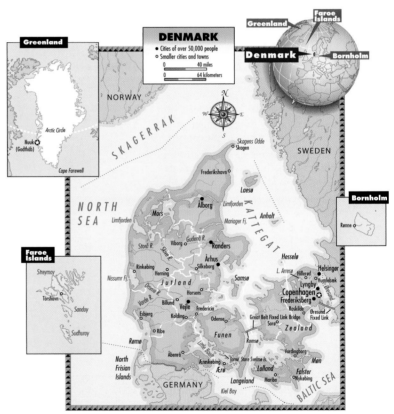

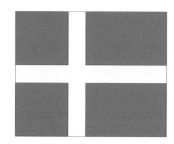

Denmark's flag

Coastal Denmark

Official religion: Evangelical Lutheran Church

National anthem: "There Is a Lovely Land" celebrates the country itself and is the anthem most often heard; "King Christian Stood by the Lofty Mast," the anthem of the royal family, is played during the queen's official appearances

Type of government: Constitutional monarchy

Chief of state: Queen

Head of government: Prime minister

Area: 16,629 square miles (43,069 sq km)

Latitude and longitude of geographic center: 56° north, 10° east

Land borders: Germany

Highest elevation: Yding Skovhøj, 568 feet (173 m) above sea level

Lowest elevation: Sea level at the coasts

Average temperatures: Winter temperatures average 32°F (0°C); summer temperatures average 63°F (17°C)

Average precipitation: 24 inches (61 cm) of total precipitation (rain and melted snow) each year

Population (1999 est.): 5,313,577

Population of largest cities:

Copenhagen	1.4 million
Århus	280,000
Odense	184,000
Ålborg	155,000
Esbjerg	73,000

Tivoli Gardens

Famous landmarks:
- ▶ *Little Mermaid statue*, Copenhagen
- ▶ *Tivoli Gardens amusement park*, Copenhagen
- ▶ *Kronborg Castle (also called Hamlet's Castle)*, Helsingør, Zealand
- ▶ *Amalienborg Palace (the queen's official home)*, Copenhagen
- ▶ *Legoland*, near Billund, Jutland
- ▶ *Cliffs of Møn*, Møn
- ▶ *Hans Christian Anderson house*, Odense, Funen

Industry: Processed food, textiles, chemical goods, electronics, furniture, wood products, ships, windmill technology

Currency: The Danish krone (DK). Common DK bills come in denominations of 50, 100, 200, 500, and 1000; in the year 2002 the currency exchanged at the rate of about 8 DK to US$1.

Weights and measures: Metric system

Literacy rate: 100 percent

Common Danish words and phrases:

Hygge	Having a good time with friends
Fodbold	Soccer
Fastelavn	Danish version of Halloween
Smørrebrød	Danish traditional open-faced sandwiches
Penge	Money

Currency

Football, or soccer

Hans Christian Andersen

Morgenmad	Breakfast
Frokost	Lunch
Middag	Dinner
Brød	Bread
Strand	Beach
Slot	Castle
Vaskeri	Laundry
Souvenirbutik	Souvenir shop
Fotohandel	Camera shop

Famous Danes:

Hans Christian Andersen (1805–1875)
Writer and storyteller

Karen Blixen (Isak Dinesen) (1885–1962)
Writer

Niels Bohr (1885–1962)
Atomic scientist

Tycho Brahe (1546–1601)
Astronomer

Erik Bruhn (1928–1986)
Ballet dancer

Kristoffer Vilhelm Eckersberg (1783–1853)
*Painter, sometimes called the
Father of Danish Art*

N.F.S. Grundtvig (1783–1872)
Clergyman and philosopher

Søren Aabye Kierkegaard (1813–1855)
Religious philosopher

Carl Nielsen (1865–1931)
Musician and composer

Queen Margrethe II (1940–)
Queen of Denmark

To Find Out More

Nonfiction

▶ Burch, Joann. *A Fairy-Tale Life: A Story About Hans Christian Andersen.* Minneapolis: Carolrhoda Press, 1994.

▶ Martell, Hazel. *The Vikings.* New York: Macmillan Press, 1992.

▶ Mason, Anthon. *Viking Times* (If You Were There Series). New York: Simon & Schuster, 1997.

▶ Mussari, Mark. *The Danish Americans.* New York: Chelsea House, 1988.

▶ Visual Geography Series. *Denmark In Pictures.* Minneapolis: Lerner, 1997.

Nonfiction for Older Readers

▶ Ministry of Foreign Affairs. *Denmark—An Official Handbook.* Copenhagen, 1996.

▶ Strange, Morten. *Culture Shock! Denmark.* Portland, OR: Graphic Arts Center Publishing Company, 2001.

Fiction

▶ Andersen, Hans Christian. *Little Mermaids and Ugly Ducklings: Favorite Fairy Tales by Hans Christian Andersen.* San Francisco: Chronicle Books, illustrated and reprinted in 2001.

▶ Elmer, Robert. *A Walk Through the Sea* (Young Underground Series). Rockville, MD: Bethany House, 1995.

▶ Elmer, Robert. *Into The Flames* (Young Underground Series). Rockville, MD: Bethany House, 1994.

Web Sites

▶ **The World Factbook—Denmark**
http://www.cia.gov/cia/publications/factbook/geos/da.html
Information on Denmark's geography, people, government, economy, transportation, and military.

▶ **Virtual Denmark**
http://virtualdenmark.dk/frames1.html
Interactive panoramic images for viewing such as cityscapes, nature, architecture, museums, churches, and so on.

▶ **Wonderful Copenhagen**
http://woco.dk
The official tourist site of Copenhagen. Information on Copenhagen's history, basic facts, general information, sights, and sports.

Organizations:

▶ **American-Scandinavian Foundation**
725 Park Avenue
New York, NY 10021
phone: (212) 879-9779

▶ **Danish Tourist Board**
P.O. Box 4649
Grand Central Station
New York, NY 10163
phone: (212) 885-9700

▶ **American Youth Hostels**
Hosteling International (Denmark)
733 15th Street NW, Suite 840
Washington, DC 20005
phone: (202) 783-6161

▶ **Royal Danish Embassy**
3200 Whitehaven Street, NW
Washington, DC 20008
phone: (202) 234-4300

Index

Page numbers in *italics* indicate illustrations.

Meet the Author

I'M R. CONRAD STEIN, AND I AM A WRITER OF HISTORY AND geography books for young readers. Over the years I've published more than a hundred books for Children's Press and for other companies. I was born and grew up in Chicago. At age eighteen I joined the Marine Corps and served for three years. After my discharge I attended the University of Illinois and graduated with a degree in history. I later lived in Mexico and studied at the University of Guanajuato. Before I began writing full-time, I worked as a teacher, a social worker, a truck driver, and a merchant seaman. I now live in Chicago with my wife (children's book author Deborah Kent) and our daughter, Janna. Another member of our family is a very lazy cat named Salem.

To prepare for this book, my wife and I visited Denmark. That was the fun part. We traveled through the country on trains and buses, we ate in small-town restaurants, and we talked to average Danes wherever we went. We found the Danes to be a very warm people. They have a sly sense of humor and enjoy laughing at themselves. Rarely have I met men and women so open and friendly. The only negative element of our trip is that we visited in January 2002 in the middle of a typically grim Danish winter. Oh, well. Some rain

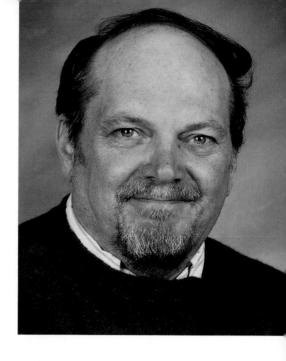

(and in Denmark's case a lot of sleet) must fall in everyone's life.

Sitting down and writing the book was, of course, the hard part. First I had to gather research material—books, Web sites, and so forth. To research and write my books I mix fact and flavor. For bare facts such as land area and population, I rely on encyclopedias. *The World Book Encyclopedia* presents facts in a clear manner. A handy Web site is the CIA World Fact Book, which is loaded with statistics. For flavor I turn to books, in this case especially those written by Danes. Flavor, to me, means the feelings behind the facts. What are the peoples' likes and dislikes? What makes the Danes laugh, and what disturbs them? One of a series, *Culture Shock! Denmark*, a book written by the Danish-born Morten Strange, was very helpful in this regard. The Web site sponsored by the Royal Danish Embassy provided a nice mixture of fact and flavor.

While writing, I dreamed of returning to the charming country of Denmark. There are bicycle trips I want to take, coastal paths I wish to hike, and museums I long to visit. Perhaps I am sentimentally attached to the country because my grandmother on my father's side was a Dane, born in southern Jutland. Sadly, that grandmother died long before I was born. My Danish roots, however vague, give me a longing to return. My wife and I are already planning a second trip to Denmark. Only this time we'll visit during June or July and avoid the Danish winter.

Photo Credits

Photographs © 2003:

A Perfect Exposure/Chili Foto & Arkiv: 67 bottom, 67 top, 71, 73, 95, 97, 112, 118, 133 top

A Perfect Exposure/Nordic Photos: 8, 13, 18 top, 18 bottom, 22, 23, 24, 27, 28, 31, 32 top, 36 bottom, 40, 43, 46, 47, 54 top, 57, 62 bottom, 64, 66, 69, 70, 72, 76, 85, 88, 90, 93, 100, 102, 119, 121, 131

AKG London: 39

AP/Wide World Photos: 126 (Henning Bagger), 53 (Joergen Jessen), 99 (Erik Johansen), 54 bottom (John McConnico), 96 (Cesar Rangel), 74 (Brian Rasmussen), 49

Bridgeman Art Library International Ltd., London/New York: 37 (Archives Charmet/Private Collection), 48 (The Stapleton Collection)

Bruce Coleman Inc.: 65 (Massimo Borchi), 30 top, 32 bottom right (J.C. Carton), 15 bottom right, 16 top right, 17, 81, 115 (Guido Cozzi), 30 bottom (Eric Dragesco), 14 (Wadigo Ferchland), 117 (Lee Foster), 33 top (Frank Krahmer), 33 bottom (John Markham), 7 bottom, 63 bottom (J. Messerschmidt), 111 (Eitan Simanor), 32 bottom left (Peter Ward)

Corbis Images: 42, 45, 107 (Bettmann), 34, 44 (Archivo Iconografico, S.A.), 108 (Bob Krist), 104 (Stephanie Maze), 29 (Tom Nebbia), 36 top (Gianni Dagli Orti), 87 (Underwood & Underwood), 101 (Bo Zaunders), 26

Dave G. Houser/HouserStock, Inc.: cover, back cover, 6, 9 (Jan Butchofsky-Houser), 52 (RDPIII)

Helga Lade Fotogentur: 7 top, 12

Image State/Len Kaufman: 62 top, 130

MapQuest.com: 131 top

Mary Evans Picture Library: 38 (Douglas McCarthy), 106, 133 bottom

Peter Arnold Inc.: 41 (P. Thompson/ Helga Lade), 68 (Still Pictures), 25 (Kevin Schafer), 16 bottom left (Tetzlaft/Lade)

R. Conrad Stein: 122

Robert Fried Photography: 80, 89

Stock Boston/Raymond Forbes: 125

The Image Works: 10, 79, 83, 84, 114, 132 bottom (Francis Dean), 78 (Sascha/Visum), 2 (Michael Thompson)

Viesti Collection, Inc.: 15 top right, 94, 113, 132 top (Diana Gleasner), 105 (Joe Viesti)

Maps by Joe LeMonnier